II

SULTAN WITHIN

İÇİMDEKİ SULTAN

SELECT POEMS OF YUNUS EMRE
In
Turkish-English

Translated By
ERSE YAGAN Also Known As Öz Yağan

SULTAN
WITHIN
    İÇİMDEKİ
    SULTAN

İslam Tasavvufunun derinliklerinde sırlı kalmış insani yaşantı hikmetlerini, en ulvi ve kıymetli bir açılım ile dile getirip yazıya döken can dostum olan Öz Yağan'a sonsuz sevgi ve saygılarımı arz ederim, teşekkürlerimi bilidiririm. Yapmış olduğu bu güncelleme çevirisi ile Yunus Emre Hz.lerinin daha iyi anlaşılabileceğini bildiğim için tekrar bu eserine teşekkürlerimi sunar okuyan tüm kardeşlerime de feyz verici olmasını temenni ederim.
Hizmet bizden, Hidayet Allah'tan.
Fakir Mehmet Şerif Çatalkaya
22.05.2020
İstanbul

    To Erse Yagan, being my life friend; who with a most divine and worthy opening brought into words and poured into writing the wisdom of human experience left hidden in the depths of Islamic Sufism, I submit my endless love and respect, I announce my thanks.
    Because I know that with this updated translation that he has done Hz. Yunus Emre will be better understood again, I offer my thanks; and for all my brothers and sisters who read it I wish that it gives enlightenment.

Service from us, Guidance from Allah
Fakir Mehmet
Şerif Çatalkaya

VIII

Table of Contents

Foreword..xix

Preface By The Author..XIX

1 Sultan Within...3
    (İçimdeki Sultan)
2 Love Is Our Minister...5
    (Aşk İmamdir Bize)
3 To Me You Are Needed..7
    (Bana Seni Gerek Seni)
4 Come See What Love Has Done To Me..............................11
    (Gel Gör Beni Aşk Neyledi)
5 Awake My Eyes..15
    (Uyan Gözlerim)
6 Just Like You They Fell...17
    (Nice Senin Gibi)
7 I Don't Die No More...19
    (Ölmezem Ayruk).
8 What Is Mortal Universe To Me..21
    (Fani Cihani Neylerim)..
9 Overwhelming Love...25
    (Aşk Başimdan Aşuban)
10 Mercy My Lord Mercy...27
    (Aman Allah'im Aman)
11 Do Not Abandon Your Heart..29
    (Hiç Vermegil Gönlünü)
12 Praise Be To God (Hallelujah) Or (Elham Dullilah)...................31
    (Elhamdülillah)
13 My Hands Are Here For Reaching You..............................35
    (Elim Sana Ermek İçin)
14 Universe Is Full Of God...37
    (Hak Cihanda Doludur)
15 I've Become Lovers With Feared One.................................39
    (Korktuğumla Yar Oldum)

16 Love Resembles A Bright Sun..........41
     (Aşk Bir Güneşe Benzer)
17 When Love Arrives Everything Old Comes To End..........45
     (Aşk Gelicek Cümle Eksikler Biter)
18 There Is An I In Me..........47
     (Bir Ben Vardir Bende)
19 See What My Lord Manifests..........49
     (Mevlam Görelim Neyler)
20 I Have Become A Friend With Friend..........51
     (Dost İle Dost Olmuşam)
21 La Ilahe Illallah..........53
     (La Ilahe İllallah)
22 Fill Me With Worship Of You..........57
     (Şöyle Hayran Eyle Beni)
23 Meaning Of Actual Truth..........61
     (Hakikatin Manasin)
24 Crazy Dervish..........63
     (Derviş Olan Kişiler Deli Olagan)
25 Chanting Lord's Name..........65
     (Tevhid Etmek)
26 One Must Hold On To Skirt Of Love..........67
     (Aşk Eteğin Tutmak Gerek)
27 The Love Of My Lord..........69
     (Ol Çalabumun Aşki)
28 Thanks And Gratitude Be To God..........71
     (Şükür Minnet Ol Allaha)
29 Hear Me O Sublime People..........73
     (İşitin Ey Ulu Kişi)
30 That Which Keeps You From 75
     (Seni Hak'dan Yiğan)
31 Such A Heart Lord Has Given Me..........77
     (Hak Bir Gönül Virdi Bana)
32 In Early Dawn I Reached Graveyard..........81
     (Sabahin Sinleye Vardum)
33 The Lot Of Those Who Are Lovers..........83
     (Aşik Olanlarin İşi...)
34 My Heart Has Seen It Again..........85

	(Yine Seyr Eyledm)	
35	To House Of Meaning We Dove	87
	(Ma'ni Evine Daldik)	
36	Render Us	89
	(Eyle Bizi)	
37	Chanting Allah Allah	91
	(Allah Deyu Deyu)	
38	My Soul From There	93
	(Canum Ben Andan)	
39	Send Message To Lovers	95
	(Haber Eylen Aşiklara)	
40	Whoever Desires Dervish	99
	(Kim Dervişlik İster İse)	
41	Walk O Heart	103
	(Yürü Ey Gönül)	
42	Oh Heart Open Your Eyes	107
	(Eya Gönül Açgil Gözün)	
43	One Who Has Come To This World	111
	(Bu Dünyaya Gelen Kişi)	
44	I Have No Intent Of Staying Here	113
	(Bunda Benim Kararim Yok)	
45	Science Is Having Knowledge	115
	(İlim İlim Bilmektir...)	
46	I Found What I Had Desired	117
	(İstediğimi Buldum)	
47	I Used To Be Wanting God	121
	(İster İdim Allahi)	
48	Give Love And Eagerness	123
	(Aşkin Ver Şevkin Ver)	
49	The Example Of This Worl	125
	(Bu Dünyanin Misali)	
50	Why Do You Weep O Nightingale	127
	(Niçin Ağlarsin Bülbül)	
51	Do Not Injure Dervishes	129
	(İncitme Dervişleri)	
52	My Sweet Lord	133
	(Dağlar İle Taşlar İle)	

53 What's Needed 137
       (Bir Şaha Kul Olmak Gerek)
54 Seven Doors 139
       (Bu Yolda Acaib Çok)
55 Oh Sultan 143
       (Ey Padişah)
56 My Trouble Was Cure To Me 145
       (Derdim Bana Derman)
Epilogue 149

XIII

FOREWORD

I first met Erse, and heard this lovely poetry spoken, in the Rifa'i-Marufi meydan (circle) of Şerif Baba Çatalkaya. Erse learned by heart both the original Turkish poem and his inspired English translation and would, on the request of the Sheikh, gift one to the listeners. Since Erse first sparked my interest in Yunus Emre, I began a search for existing written English translations with the beauty and power of Erse's, and could find none that even approached the authenticity of these. I say "authenticity" because Yunus' teachings are the basis of Sufi teachings, and the English that some translators render doesn't adequately capture the depth and beauty of Yunus' thoughts. Erse's translations do.

As an example, I once read a translation that said "Hold on to the hand of a striding hero", which Erse instead translates to the much closer actual words of "Hold on to the skirt of an attained one". This totally changes the meaning, encouraging the reader to find a true Sheikh and hold fast to his teachings. There are also depths in this translation that will only be grasped by those with a thorough understanding of Islamic thought; for example poem #13, which hearkens back to Hallaj and the "justice" that he received.

When first reading Erse's translation you may think, as I initially did, that there were mistakes in the English. Not so. Erse explained to me that he was trying very hard to give English-speakers as close to the same experience, in English, as Yunus delivers in Turkish. For example, Yunus sometimes makes up words, adding endings like "ingly" (see poem #9), and Erse is faithful to that; this is most obvious in poem #24, "Crazy Dervish". Without Erse unveiling that for us, we English-speakers would never know Yunus' playful aspect with words; I've never found any other such translation. Another example of this is poem #53 that opens, "To submit to a King's needed, Never unreachable must be" (i.e. he must be such a king that he is never unreachable). Erse has also judiciously omitted articles such as "the" or "a" to make each line the exact same number of syllables as in the Yunus Turkish spoken version. Where he could do so without sacrificing accuracy, the poems still rhyme. He also remains as true as possible to the actual Turkish meaning of words, selecting each one with the care that only a truly bilingual person, and one very well-schooled in Sufism, could ever achieve.

We are blessed to be able to publish this first edition of Erse's inspired translations, which bring Yunus intact to the English-speaking world. I hope you will enjoy the beauty and depth of Erse's translations as much as I do. They are like giving a perfect, precious jewel (Yunus' poetry) to a master jeweler, who has set it into a delicate filigree setting to showcase its beauty.

Bedi'a Roesler, June 2020

PREFACE BY THE AUTHOR

xx

Yunus Emre was an illiterate Turkish farmer who lived in 13th century, in contrast to his contemporary Rumi who was a university professor who published many volumes of poetry.

The only time that the two met and spent hours together, Rumi read his poetry to Yunus. After listening patiently for a long time, Yunus spoke: "You have said it beautifully but too long. I can say the same thing in one sentence. "When Rumi asked him what that was, Yunus said what is probably his most well known statement. "I wrapped myself in flesh and bones and appeared as Yunus."

When Rumi heard that, he said "Oh my God, I climbed this great pinnacle and found this illiterate Turkish farmer sitting there waiting for me." The wisdom and attainment of

Yunus came, not from an exterior source, but from the treasure house that exists in every human.

Yunus was illiterate, he did not write. He only recited from the heart .He spoke an uneducated, colloquial Turkish that wasn't always grammatically correct. I tried to reflect that in English. A perfect example is #7. I could translate it into perfect English, but then that wouldn't sound like Yunus. (By the way, some Yunus poems were written with a very educated Turkish, which included Arabic and Persian, because Turkish wasn't adequate for poetry. A perfect example is #6. The reason for that is that after Yunus, many poets came who were Yunus lovers, and they signed their poetry as Yunus. These got mixed up with real Yunus poems. Some say that these poets were channeling the poems that Mulla Kasim threw into the water over the bridge. Another example is # 52, Daglar Ile, Taslar Ile.)

When translating Yunus I tried as much as I could, without sacrificing the content, to reflect his style of writing. That worked better with some poems than others. I asked myself, how would Yunus say it if he said it in English. . When I first met Sherif Baba I read to him "Just Like You They Fell" (#6 in this book). Each line has the same number of syllables and every other line ends with the same word. This was the style that Sufi poets used in those days. He said: "You have made Yunus speak in English."

It has been almost twenty years since then, and lately people have been urging me to publish. I thought perhaps it is time I made an offering and shared these gems.

I was born to a Moslem family and was a devout Moslem till I was fourteen years old. In the early 60's I got baptized and became a Christian when my father became a Christian. My father was disappointed with the Islamic world. He had a background in Sufism and was a scholar. He loved poetry, especially Sufi poetry. I could say he jump started my interest in poetry. He believed, as I do, that Sufism represents Islam the best. When he came to know Jesus, he believed that Jesus was the greatest dervish that ever lived. Dervishood has three pillars according to Sherif Baba. Love of God, beautiful morals, and service to humanity. Jesus loved God so much that he would rather die for God than kill in the name of God. My father did not urge any of his children to become Christian. He gave us total freedom to choose, but when we saw the change in our father after he met Jesus we wanted to follow.

I was a devout Christian till I was sixteen years old, at which time I became disappointed with mainstream Christianity and I came to the conclusion that God was a man-made concept that is used as a crutch, and there is no God up there. I became an atheist.

In my early 20's I got into Yoga and read Bhagavat Gita. Then I realized that there indeed is a God, but not up in the sky but within us. Any of you who have read Bhagavat Gita will remember the picture of Lord Krishna looking like a sultan with a turban, within everybody's heart.

What drew me to Yunus was the first poem in this book, Sultan Within.

When I read Yunus' Sultan Within, I thought, Oh my God, Yunus was illiterate yet he sounds like he read Bhagavat Gita. I was drawn to Yunus' poetry and was amazed to find in his poetry the same basic principles that are taught in yogic philosophy. This is not surprising when one considers that there is only one truth, one reality throughout the universe. Any philosophy that touches that truth will be speaking of the same reality.

Those of you who are familiar with "yoga" know that it means to yoke, to join together. It is based on the premise that we humans live in a world of false perception, a duality.

We have a false self called the ego created by the intellect. Ego is our sense of separateness from everything else, a sense of individuality. In reality there is only one thing in the universe, call it whatever you like. That one thing becomes everything else. The individual ego dies when the body dies. However there is a more permanent part of us that lives beyond the physical death. This true self which some people call the higher self and which I like to call Beingness is always blissful, needs nothing and is the source of everything. It is the ego that laughs, cries and has desires.

The purpose of yoga is to dissolve the ego into the Beingness and be one. It has been called dying and being born again. The purpose of human life is to realize the Beingness within. When the ego becomes aware of its separateness a desire develops to reunite with The Beingness.

The gateway that brings the Beingness to the lower self is the heart, that is the heart chakra. But the heart has to be touched by love and opened. A closed heart does not allow entry. When the ego is in love, it is being same as the Beingness whose nature is love, therefore the gate opens. The shift of awareness from the lower self to Beingness is instant because it does not require the use of the body or the mind. In fact it cannot be done with the mind. If you try you will sink more into the lower self. But because it does not require the use of the body or the mind, the lower self does not change instantly although the shift in awareness is instant. However, the process that transforms the lower self begins instantly. It is like the Beingness is an endless ocean of warm water and the lower self is a finite block of ice. They are made of the same thing but one is endless, warm and soft, the other finite, hard and cold. As long as they are apart the block of ice remains as such. When the gateway opens and the warm water engulfs the ice, the ice does not melt instantly but the melting process begins instantly. Eventually it dissolves and is part of the ocean. This dissolving process is a very difficult period for the ego because it is slowly dying, but the ego endures because of the pull of love.

"Come see what love has done to me." (#4 in this book)

The root reason for the heart to remain closed and difficult to enter is that we humans come from generations and generations of warriors. If you look at human history there has always been battles and wars. We have a cellular memory of this, warrior genes if you will. As Yunus says in the first poem:

"The inner sanctum of that sultan has all of seven doorways, (the seven chakras).

To take a stroll through all seven ,I have deep yearning for.

At every door a person with hundred thousand soldiers."

Could he be talking about the warrior genes? And what overcomes these warrior genes?

He goes on to say:

" With sword of love to break all I have a deep yearning for."

What a metaphor, using love as a sword! It is the only thing that works against warrior genes.

In Yunus Emre's poetry the Beingness is referred to at times as "sultan within", at other times as "dost" or "friend." Ego is called "nefs". Ego is motivated by desire and pleasure. We humans are creatures of desire. We go where our most prominent desire takes us. Since the Beingness or "Lord within" is always blissful, lacks nothing and is the source of everything, any glimpse the ego may get of it, is associated with the sweetest bliss and pleasure. This is the reason why a lot of people find deep satisfaction in meditation. If the ego is made to be silent even for a moment we are in the presence of the true self whose natural state is that of bliss.

When the ego gets a taste of this bliss, this "Divine Nectar" it falls in love with it and is motivated in that direction. This love of the Divine becomes the most important thing in one's life. That is why mystic poets are called "ashik" or "lover".

The presence within is referred to as "Beloved". The greatest pleasure in life the ego can taste is Divine Nectar, and the greatest desire the ego can have is to unite, to be one with Sultan Within.

This divine love "ashk" is like a fire that burns off all bad habits the ego has developed throughout life. Since ego is motivated by pleasure, in order to give up all our bad habits that are associated with pleasure we must have a greater pleasure with which to replace them. Divine Nectar is such a pleasure.

"Nectar descending from God, we have drunk Hallelujah." (# 12 in this book.)

Note: This book is meant for people who speak English, who may be Christian, Jewish, or Moslem. Christians and Jews may prefer Hallelujah and Moslems may prefer Elhamdulillah. If a person thinks that one is better than the other, that person is part of a collective ego, because they mean the same thing. Praise be to God. We have to come to a place where Elhamdulillah and Hallelujah are one and the same.

This bliss can be reached by chanting God's name in any shape or form.

In Sufism it is known as "zikr". In yoga it is known as bakhta yoga. Masters claim that in our day and age when evil forces are doing their worst, it is the only sure and safe form of yoga.

Yunus was a great advocate of this. He claimed that bliss and attainment could be reached through zikr. His poetry has a very powerful instigating and guiding quality. One can easily love it and be guided by it.

I love Jesus, but I am not a Christian. I love Mohammed, but I am not a Moslem. I love Moses, but I am not Jewish. I am beyond religion and I embrace all religion. That is what I love about Yunus. He includes all and he embraces all.

"Like Jesus I gave up the earth, I am traversing the heavens. I have become the face of Moses..." (# 8 in this book)

"We don't say any faith is contrary to ours. From core of all religion is born true love." (# 2 in this book)

"The Torah and The Bible, The Koran and The Zebur,

And the commandments in these, all in the body we found" (# 35)

The main theme in all Yunus' poetry is having a love affair with God within, who is often called The Beloved.

I offer these translations together with the Turkish versions back to back, with the hope that you can derive the same satisfaction, bliss and guidance that I have found in them.

God Bless.

Oz Yagan

SELEC POEMS OF YUNUS EMRE
In
Turkish-English

-1-

İÇİMDEKİ SULTAN

Bu vücûdun şehrine her dem giresim gelir
İçimdeki Sultan'ın yüzün göresim gelir

İşidirim sözünü göremezsem yüzünü
Yüzünü görmekliğe canım veresim gelir

O sultan halvetinin yedi kapısı vardır
Yedisinden içeri cevlan urasım gelir

Her kapıda bir kişi yüz bin çerisi ile
Aşk kılıcın kuşanıp cümle kırasım gelir

Erenlerin sohbeti artırır ma'rifeti
Cahilleri sohbetten her dem kovasım gelir

Dost geldi bana mihman bunca yıl bunca zaman
Gerçek İsmail'leyin kurban olasım gelir

Erenlerin nazarı toprağı gevher eder
Erenler kademinde toprak olasım gelir

Miskin Yunus'un nefsi dört tabiat içinde
Aşk ile can sırrına Pinhan olasım gelir

SULTAN WITHIN

To enter this body's city, I have a deep yearning for.
To see face of Sultan within, I have a deep yearning for.

I can hear his lovely words, cannot see his countenance,
To give my life to see his face, I have a deep yearning for.

Inner sanctum of that Sultan has all of seven doorways.*
To take a stroll through all seven, I have a deep yearning for.

At every door a person with hundred thousand soldiers,
With sword of love to break all, I have a deep yearning for.

The sohbet** of the attained adds to one's ability,
To chase the ignorant from sohbet, I have a deep yearning for.

Friend came to me as a guest for all of these years and time,
To be sacrificed like Ishmail, I have a deep yearning for.

The glance of the attained turns dirt into precious stone,
To be dirt in the realm of the attained, I have a deep yearning for.

Ego of humble Yunus in four corners of nature,
With love to keep secret of soul, I have a deep yearning for.

*the seven chakras
**sohbet: conversation about God in the circle of the attained.

- 2 -

AŞK İMAMDIR BİZE

Aşk imamdır bize gönül cemaat
Kıblemiz dost yüzü daimdir salat

Gönül secde kılar dost mihrabına
Yüzün yere vurup kılar münacat

Beş namaz tertibi bir vakte geldi
Beş bölük oluben kim kıla taat

Şeriat der sakın şartı bırakma
Şart şol kişiyedir kim ola hiyanet

Doğruluk bekleyen dost eşiğinde
Gümansız olur ana ilahi devlet

Bir kimse dinine hilaf demeniz
Din tamam olacak doğar muhabbet

Dost yüzün görücek şirk yağmalandı
Onun için kapıda kaldı şeriat

Yunus öyle esirdir dost eşiğinde
Diyeler kurtulmaya ezel ü ebet

- 2 -

LOVE IS OUR MINISTER

Love is our minister, our flock is the heart.
Our direction face of Friend, our worship constant.

The heart prostrates itself to the Lord within,
With face pressed on the ground it is praying.

The five prayer times are gathered into one,
Who can perform worship divided by five.

The Dogma says never to abandon law.
The laws are for those with treachery at heart.

Those who guard righteousness at Friend's threshold,
Will undoubtedly attain Kingdom of God.

We don't say any faith is contrary to ours.
From core of all religion is born true love.

Seeing the Friend's face, duality we rout.
It is for this reason The Dogma is out.

Yunus, such a captive at Friend's threshold,
May it be said that he remain so for good.

- 3 -

BANA SENİ GEREK SENİ

Aşkın aldı benden beni
Bana seni gerek, seni
Ben yanarım dün ü gün ü
Bana seni gerek, seni

Ne varlığa sevinirim
Ne yokluğa yerinirim
Aşkın ile avunurum
Bana seni gerek, seni

Aşkın aşıklar öldürür
Aşk denizine daldırır
Tecellisiyle doldurur
Bana seni gerek, seni

Aşkın şarabından içem
Mecnun olup dağa düşem
Sensin dün ü gün endişem
Bana seni gerek, seni

Aşıklara sohbet gerek
Zahit'lere cennet gerek
Mecnunlara Leyla gerek
Bana seni gerek, seni

Eğer beni öldüreler
Külüm göğe savuralar
Toprağım onda çağıra
Bana seni gerek, seni

TO ME YOU ARE NEEDED

Your love took me away from me,
To me you are needed, you are.
I am burning day in day out,
To me you are needed, you are.

Neither am I happy to have,
Nor am I unhappy to lack,
I am consoled by your sweet love
To me you are needed, you are.

The love of you slays lovers,
Makes one dive into love's ocean,
Fills one with manifestation,
To me you are needed, you are.

Let me drink from the wine of love,
Be Majnun* and fall on mountains,
You are my care day in day out,
To me you are needed, you are.

Lovers of God need the sohbet**,
And the pious need paradise,
The lovers need the beloved,
To me you are needed, you are.

And if ever they should slay me,
Cast my ashes up in the sky,
Let my dust call out in a cry,
To me you are needed, you are.

Cennet cennet dedikleri
Bir ev ile bir kaç huri
İsteyene ver onları
Bana seni gerek, seni

Yunus dürür benim adım
Dün gün artar benim odum
İki cihanda maksudum
Bana seni gerek, seni

What is known as the paradise ,
Celestial women in a house,
Give them to who ever desires,
To me you are needed, you are.

Yunus is what is called my name,
Every day adds to my flame,
In both universes I claim,
To me you are needed, you are.

*From Leila and Majnun, also means devastated
**Conversation in the circle of the attained

- 4 -

GEL GÖR BENİ AŞK NEYLEDİ

Ben yürürüm yane yane
Aşk boyadı beni kane
Ne akılım ne divane
Gel gör beni aşk neyledi

Kah eserim yeller gibi
Kah tozarım yerler gibi
Kah akarım seller gibi
Gel gör beni aşk neyledi

Akan su gibi çağlarım
Dertli yüreğim dağlarım
Yârim için ben ağlarım
Gel gör beni aşk neyledi

Ben yürürüm ilden il'e
Dost sorarım dilden dile
Gurbette halim kim bile
Gel gör beni aşk neyledi

Gurbet elinde yürürüm
Dostu düşümde görürüm
Uyanır melul olurum
Gel gör beni aşk neyledi

Benzim sarı gözlerim yaş
Bağrım yare ciğerim taş
Halim bilen dertli kardeş
Gel gör beni aşk neyledi

- 4 -

COME SEE WHAT LOVE HAS DONE TO ME

Burning, burning I walk and wade,
Your love has dyed me to blood red,
Neither am I sane nor am mad,
Come see what love has done to me.

One moment like the wind I blow,
One moment I dust like the earth,
One moment like the flood I flow,
Come see what love has done to me.

Like the flowing water I splash,
My heart full of sorrow I thrash,
For Beloved I weep and lash,
Come see what love has done to me.

I wander from realm to realm,
I ask for Friend from tongue to tongue,
Who knows my state in foreign land,
Come see what love has done to me.

I am walking in strangers' land,
In my dreams I visit the Friend,
I awake and feel so despaired,
Come see what love has done to me.

My color pale my eyes teary,
My bosom bare my heart dreary,
Only troubled brother sees me,
Come see what love has done to me.

Aşkın beni mest eyledi
Aldı gönlüm hast eyledi
Öldürmeye kasd eyledi
Gel gör beni aşk neyledi

Ben Yunus-ı biçareyim
Aşk elinden avareyim
Baştan ayağa yareyim
Gel gör beni aşk neyledi

Your love has made me ecstatic,
Took my heart and made me lovesick,
It has set out to slay me,
Come see what love has done to me.

I am Yunus, full of sorrow,
I am wandering in love's woe,
I am wounded from head to toe,
Come see what love has done to me.

- 5 -

UYAN GÖZLERİM

Ömür bahçesinin gülü dolmadan
Uyan gel gözlerim gafletten uyan
Ecel bir gün bize haydi demezsen
Uyan gel gözlerim gafletten uyan

Niçin gaflet ile mağrur olursun
Geçer kervan gider yolda kalırsın
Be vallahi sonra pişman olursun
Uyan gel gözlerim gafletten uyan

Kaba döşekte yatma döne döne
Olup mağrur uyuma kana kana
İletirler seni karangu sine
Uyan gözlerim gafletten uyan

Yunus artık yeter sözün tutulmaz
Senin kumaşların burda satılmaz
Yunus yatmak ile dosta gidilmez
Uyan gel gözlerim gafletten uyan

AWAKE MY EYES

Before the rose of the garden of life fades,
Wake my eyes come on and from ignorance wake.
Before death arrives one day "come on" it says,
Wake my eyes, come on and from ignorance wake.

Why do you so proudly ignorance retain,
Passing caravan leaves, on road you remain,
And God knows that you will feel remorse and pain,
Wake my eyes, come on and from ignorance wake.

On such a puffy bed do not toss and turn,
Oh do not be so proud and sleep on and on,
They will put you down to a darkened grave then,
Wake my eyes, come on and from ignorance wake.

Yunus enough already your words aren't heard,
Your garments and goods here they cannot be sold.
Yunus by sleeping you do not get to Friend*,
Wake, my eyes, come on and from ignorance wake.

*Lord within

-6-

NİCE SENİN GİBİ

Cemalin pertevi gülzara düştü
Ki şevkinden bülbüller zare düştü

Şarabı Aşkın İçelden bu gönlüm
Zeber abad olup mestane düştü

Devasın sormuşun derdim tabibe
Dedi derdin senin biçare düştü

Kul olsun pare pare riyze riyze
Gönül kim sencileyin yare düştü

Cemali şem'ine yandınmı Yunus
Nice senin gibi pervane düştü.

-6-

JUST LIKE YOU THEY FELL

The light of your beauty on rose garden fell.
From exuberance, nightingales to a whisper fell.

Since my heart has drunk from the wine of your love,
Into highest intoxication it fell.

I asked the doctor for cure of my trouble.
He said your trouble into hopelessness fell.

Let the servant of God be cut in pieces,
Ever since my heart with you in love it fell.

Did you burn in candle of beauty Yunus,
Many a moth before just like you they fell.

- 7 -

ÖLMEZEM AYRUK

Ağla gözüm ağla gülmesem ayruk
Gönül dosta gider gelmezem ayruk

Ne gam bunda bana bin kez ölürsem
Anda ölüm olmaz ölmezem ayruk

Yansın canım yansın Aşkın od'una
Aksın kanlı yaşım silmezem ayruk

Göyündüm aşk ile ta kül olunca
Boyandım rengine solmazam ayruk

Beni irşad eden mürşid-i kamil
Yeter bir el dahi almazam ayruk

Varlığım yokluğa denişmişem ben
Bugün cana başa kalmazam ayruk

Fenaden bakiye göç eyler olduk
Yöneldim şol yola dönmezem ayruk

Muhabbet bahrinin gavvası oldum
Gerekmez Ceyhun'a Dalmazam ayruk

Söyler aşık dilinden bunu Yunus
Kaçan aşık isem ölmezem ayruk

- 7 -

I DON'T DIE NO MORE

Cry O my eyes cry, I do not laugh no more,
My heart goes to Friend, I do not come no more.

No regrets if I die for a thousand times,
There is no death in him, I don't die no more.

Burn my soul burn ever in the fire of Ashk.*
Let my hurting tears flow, I don't care no more.

I have burned with love till I became ashes,
I am in your colour, I don't fade no more.

The one that's guiding me is an attained one,
Is good enough for me, I don't need no more.

I have traded all my wealth for poverty.**
Now I have no need for mundane care no more.

Mortal to infinite we are migrating,
I am on that road, I don't return no more.

I have become diver of the sea of love,
There's no need to dive into river no more.

From the tongue of lover tells this now Yunus,
If I am a lover of God, I don't die no more.

*Ashk: Divine Love
** This can also be translated as: I have traded my ego into nothingness

- 8 -

FANİ CİHANI NEYLERİM

Mülk-i bekadan gelmişem
Fani cihanı neylerim
Ben dost Cemal'in görmüşem
Nur u cihanı neylerim

Vahdet meyinin cür'asın
Ma'şuk elinden işmişem
Ben dost kokusun almışam
Misk-i Hıta'nı neylerim

İsa gibi yeri koyup
Gökleri seyran eylerim
Musa'yı didar olmuşam
Ben "lenterani" neylerim

Eyyübleyin maşukumun
Cevrin tahammül eyledim
Cercisleyin Hak yoluna
Çıkmayan canı neylerim

İbrahim'im Cebrail'e
Hiç ihtiyacım kalmadı
Muhammed'im dosta giden
Ben tercümanı neylerim

İsmailim Hak yoluna
Can'ımı kurban eyledim
Çünkü bu can kurban sana
Ben Koç kurbanı neylerim

WHAT IS MORTAL UNIVERSE TO ME

I've come from infinite estate,
What's mortal universe to me.
I've seen beauty of Lord within,
What is light of heavens to me.

The mouthful of drink of oneness
I've drunk from hand of Beloved.
I got a whiff of the scent of Friend,
What is scent of perfume to me.

Like Jesus I gave up the earth,
I am traversing the heavens.
I've become the face of Moses,
What is "Lenterani"* to me.

Like Job I have born with patience
The torment of my Beloved.
Like St. George** on the road to God,
What's unslayable life to me.

I am Abraham, for Gabriel
I have no more need remaining.
I'm Mohammed on way to Friend,
What is interpreter to me.

I'm Ishmail for the sake of God
I offered my life sacrifice.
For this life is offered to you,
What's sacrificial ram to me.

Aşık Yunus ma'şuk ile
Vuslat bulunca mest olur
Ben şişeyi vurdum taşa
Namus u arı neylerim

Ashik*** Yunus with Beloved
When united finds ecstasy.
I broke the bottle against the rock,
What is shame or honor to me.

*'Lenterani"; A verse from Koran meaning "You cannot see me." When Moses asked God to show his face to him, God said: "Look at what happens to this mountain when I show my face to it." Moses looked at the mountain which was leveled to the ground. Moses was overwhelmed and withdrew his request.
**St. George: It is believed that he was a prophet who came after Jesus who was slain several times and each time came alive again.
***Ashik: Lover of God

- 9 -

AŞK BAŞIMDAN AŞUBAN

Giderim ben aşk başımdan aşuban
Yanarak aşk od'una tutuşuban

Dost içimde od bıraktı yandım
Gece gündüz aşk ile dolaşuban

Ne var eğer aşkdan yandım ise
Yanmadı kim aşk ile uğraşuban

Aşık olgil ma'şukun didarına
Ma'şuk olgil aşk ile sarmaşuban

Ver Yunus canın bugün şükraneye
Kimseler bulmaz yârin isteyüban

OVERWHELMING LOVE

I am going with love overwhelmingly,
Burning in the fire of love flamingly.

Friend left such a fire in me and I burned,
Day and night with divine love wanderingly.

What of it if I am burned in fire of love,
Who's not burned in fire of love involvingly.

Go ahead be a lover of Beloved's face,
Become beloved with love entangledly.

Yunus give your life today with gratitude,
Tomorrow no one can find it wantingly.

- 10 -

AMAN ALLAH'IM AMAN

Alman tenden canımı
Aman Allah'ım aman
Görmeden cananımı
Aman Allah'ım aman

Bir kez nurun göreyim
Payine yüz süreyim
Canım onda vereyim
Aman Allah'ım aman

Ahım göğe çıkmasın
Melekleri yakmasın
Felekleri yıkmasın
Aman Allah'ım aman

Zar eyleme işimi
Zehr eyleme aşımı
Dökme kanlı yaşımı
Aman Allah'ım aman

Yunus canın şükrana
Kurban etsin canana
Atma daim hicrana
Aman Allah'ım aman

- 10 -

MERCY MY LORD MERCY

Take not my soul from body,
Mercy O my Lord mercy.
Before I see my beloved,
Mercy O my Lord mercy.

For once may I see your light,
And rub my face on your feet,
And then surrender my soul,
Mercy O my Lord mercy.

Let not my sigh reach the sky,
Set aflame all the angels,
Demolish all the heavens,
Mercy O my Lord mercy.

Make not my work difficult,
Make not my meal poison
O, shed not my blood and tears,
Mercy O my Lord mercy.

Yunus his life thankfully,
Sacrificed to Beloved.
Cast not my heart to bitterness,
Mercy O my Lord Mercy.

- 11 -

HİÇ VERMEGİL GÖNLÜNÜ

Hiç vermegil gönlünü dünyaya ine bir gün
Dünyaya gönül veren düşe zulmüne bir gün

Bu dünya bir urandır ademiler yutucu
Uş dahi bize gele yuta toyuna bir gün

Ol kuşun yuvasıyım doğan yanında ola
O da elbet vurulur ok u yay ile bir gün

Miskin biçare Yunus tut erenler eteğin
Ol sen Hakk'a ilete düşgil suna bir gün

- 11 -

DO NOT ABANDON YOUR HEART

Do not ever abandon your heart to this world one day.
One who gives heart to the world falls to oppression one day.

This world is such a trap that consumes Adam's descendants,
That will come to consume even us in a feast one day.

The nest of that bird I am, that the falcon perched beside,
It too will surely be hit with bow and arrow one day.

Poor wretched Yunus do cling to the skirt of the attained,
It will reach you to the Lord, it will manifest one day.

- 12 -

ELHAMDÜLİLLAH

Hak'tan inen şerbeti
İçtik elhamdülillah
Şu kudret denizini
Geçtik elhamdülillah

Şu karşıki dağları
O yemyeşil bağları
Sağlık şifalık ile
Aştık elhamdülillah

Beri gel barışalım
Yadisen bilişelim
Atımız eyerlendi
Koştuk elhamdülillah

Kuru iken yaş olduk
Ayak iken baş olduk
Kanatlandık kuş olduk
Uçtuk elhamdülillah

Vardığımız illerde
Şol safalı yollarda
Baba Tapduk manasın
Aldık elhamdülillah

Geçtik yazı kısladık
Çok hayırlar işledik
Üş bahar oldu geri
Göçtük elhamdülillah

- 12 -

PRAISE BE TO GOD (HALLELUJAH) or (ELHAMDULLILAH)

Nectar descending from God,
We have drunk hallelujah.
This great ocean of power,
We have passed hallelujah.

Over all yonder mountains,
And all these green vineyards,
With safety and sanity,
Over passed hallelujah.

Come over let us make up,
If stranger let us meet up.
Our horses have been saddled,
We have run hallelujah.

From dry we have become fresh.
From feet we have become head.
On wings we have become birds.
We have flown hallelujah.

In the realms we arrived,
On the roads that we delight,
Meaning of Father Tapduk,*
We attained hallelujah.

Summer passed the winter came,
Many good deeds we did claim,
Now three more springs have passed by,
We returned hallelujah.

Taptuğun tapusunda
Kul olduk kapısında
Yunus miskin çiğ idik
Piştik elhamdülillah

On estate of Tapduk's land,
At his door servant we stand.
Yunus, poor novice we were,
We matured hallelujah.

*Tapduk: Yunus Emre's spiritual master

- 13 -

ELİM SANA ERMEK İÇİN

Elim sana ermek için gözüm seni görmek için
Bunda sana verem canım anda seni bulmak için

Bunda canım verdim sana anda ıvaz ne veresin
Etme ıvaz Uçmağ'ını söylemezem uçmak için

Uçmak uçmağım dediğin benim ile eğlendiğin
Bir acı ile bir huri yok hevesim kaçmak için

Zahidlere vergil onu ben isterim yanlız seni
Ayırmagıl senden beni Ab-ı Kevser ırmak için

Yunus aşık oldu sana didarını göster bana
Eğer zulüm etmez isen dad eylegil müştaak için

- 13 -

MY HANDS ARE HERE FOR REACHING YOU

My hands are here for reaching you,
My eyes are here for seeing you,
Let me offer you my life here,
In afterlife for finding you.

I have given you my life here,
In afterlife what do you give.
Do not offer me your heaven,
I say this not for the heaven.

What you call heaven my heaven,
The one with which you are teasing,
A house with heavenly women,
No desire have I for running.

Go ahead and give to pious,
All I desire is only you.
Do not separate me from you,
For river of heavenly water.

Yunus fallen in love with you,
Show your beautiful face to me.
If you do not give much suffering,
Give your justice for the longing.

- 14 -

HAK CİHANDA DOLUDUR

Hak cihanda doludur
Kimseler Hakk'ı bilmez
Kendin ne istesen de
Ol senden ayrı olmaz

Ahret yolu ıraktır
Doğruluk key yeraktır
Ayrılık pek fıraktır
Hiç giden geri gelmez

Dünya benimdir dersin
Dünyaya el sunarsın
Niçin yalan söylersin
Hiç sen dediğin olmaz

Hep bir şerbetten içer
Dünyaya gelen göçer
Hemen bir köprü geçer
Cahiller anı bilmez

Gelin danışık edelim
İşin ona din tutalım
Sevelim söyliyelim
Bu dünya kese kalmaz

Yunus söz anlar isen
Manayı dinler isen
Sana amel geretir
Bunda hiç kimse kalmaz

- 14 -

UNIVERSE IS FULL OF GOD

Universe is full of God,
Yet no one seems to know God.
Regardless of what you want
He does not remain apart.

Way to afterlife is far,
Truthfulness is best tool,
Separateness is painful,
Those who go never return.

You say that this world is yours,
And you reach out with your hands,
Why is it you tell such lies,
What you want comes not to pass.

All drink from the same sherbet,
All who come to world leave it,
So quickly they cross a bridge,
The ignorant don't know it.

Come on and let us consult,
Let us find a way to God,
With love in heart let us say,
In this world no one will stay.

Yunus if you understand,
You listen and comprehend,
What you need is to strive on,
For no one gets to stay on.

- 15 -

KORKTUĞUMLA YAR OLDUM

Nitekim ben beni bildim, yakın bil kim Hak'kı buldum
Hakkı buluncaydı korktum, şimdi korkudan kurtuldum
Ayruk düşünmez korkmazam, bir zerrece kayurmazam
Ben şimdi kimden korkayım, korktuğum ile yar oldum
Azrail gelmez canıma, sorucu gelmez sınime
Bunlar beni ne sorsunlar, anı sorduran ben oldum
Ya ben onca kaçan olam, ol buyruğunu buyuram
Ol geldi gönlüme doldu, ben ana bir kan oldum
Aşklılar bizden alalar, aşksızlar hot ne bileler
Kimler ala kimler vere, ben bir ulu dükkan oldum
Yunus'a Hak açtı kapu, Yunus Hak'ka kıldı tapu
Baki devlet benimkiymiş, ben kul iken sultan oldum

- 15 -

I'VE BECOME LOVERS WITH FEARED ONE

Since I have come to know myself, know for certain that I have known God.
My fears were till I have found him, now free of fear I have become.

I think not of fear anymore, I do not worry the least bit.
Of whom should I be afraid now, lovers with feared one I've become.

Angel of death comes not for me; the asker comes not to my grave.
Of what should he interrogate, the one that sends him I've become.

And he and I have become The One, his will and mine have become one.
He has come and has filled my heart, a spring of his I have become.

Those who have love will gain from us, those without love know no better.
Who will give and who will receive, a great storehouse I have become.

To Yunus Lord opened the door, Yunus paid worship to the Lord.
Infinite kingdom became mine, from servant, Sultan I've become.

- 16 -

AŞK BİR GÜNEŞE BENZER

Ey yarenler işidin
Aşk bir güneşe benzer
Aşık olmayan gönül
Bir katı taşa benzer

Taş gönülde ne biter
Dilinde ağu tüter
Nice yumşak söylese
Sözü savaşa benzer

Aşka versen gönlünü
Yumuşar muma döner
Taş gönül kararmıştır
Key kati kışa benzer

Münkir işini bilmez
İşi ileri gelmez
Nice tabir olunsun
Anlamaz düşe benzer

Hırs anı almışdürür
Nefsine kalmışdürür
Kendi tatlı canına
Yavuz yoldaşa benzer

Aşık canı dölenmez
Ta dosta varmayınca
Dünyada kararı yok
Pervazlı kuşa benzer

LOVE RESEMBLES A BRIGHT SUN

Hear me now my dear loved ones:
A bright sun, love resembles.
A heart that does not know love,
A hard boulder resembles.

What can grow on a stone heart?
Poison smolders on its tongue,
However softly spoken,
Battle ground it resembles.

If you give your heart to love,
Turns into a soft candle.
Heart of stone is a dark one,
Severe winter resembles.

Denier knows not his business,
His affairs know no progress,
No matter how instructed,
Nonsense nightmare resembles.

He's taken over by greed.
Ego's victim he remains,
To his very own sweet soul,
Bad companion resembles.

Soul of lover gives no fruit
Till it reaches Beloved.
A transient in this world,
Bird in a cage resembles.

Aşık canı katlanmaz
Dosta ulaşmak ister
Nice katlansın buna
Misali boşa gider

Yunus geç endişeden
Ne gerek bu pişeden
Ere aşk gerek övdün
Andan dervişe benzer

Lover's soul does not put up,
Wants to reach the Lord Within.
How would it put up with this,
A lost cause it resembles.

Yunus drop anxiety,
No need for society,
The attained need to have love,
That's what dervish resembles.

AŞK GELİCEK CÜMLE EKSİKLER BİTER

Nolur ise ko ki olsun nolusar
Yeter ki gönül Mevlayı bulsun nolusar
Aşk denizi gene taşmış kan akar
Aşık-ı bi çare dalsın nolusar
Bu denize düşen ölür dediler
Ölür ise ko ki ölsün nolusar
Aşk gelicek cümle eksikler biter
Bitmez ise ko ki kalsın nolusar
Akıbet şol göze toprak dolusar
Bir gün öndün, ko ki dolsun nolusar
Dünyanın mansıplariyle izzetin
Yunus kodu alan alsın nolusar

WHEN LOVE ARRIVES EVERYTHING OLD COMES TO END

Whatever happens let it happen, so what.
So long as the heart finds Beloved, so what.

The ocean of love overflows, treasure flows.
Let the poor wretched lover dive in, so what.

They say the one who falls in this ocean dies.
If he dies, let him go ahead die, so what.

When love arrives everything old comes to end.
Anything that does not end, let it stay, so what.

And in the end these eyes will be filled with dirt.
Let them become filled a day sooner, so what.

All these worldly things are the ones respected.
Yunus gave up, whoever wants let him take, so what.

- 18 -

BİR BEN VARDIR BENDE

Severim seni candan içeru
Yolum vardır erkandan içeru
Şeriat, tarikat yoldur varana
Hakikat meyvası andan içeru
Dinin terk edenin küfürüdür işi
Ol ne küfürdür, imandan içeru
Beni bende demen, bende değilim
Bir ben vardır, benden içeru
Beni benden alana ermez elim
Kim kadem basa Sultandan içeru
Süleyman kuş dilin bilir dediler
Süleyman var, Sülayman'dan içeru
Tecelliden nasip erdi kimine
Kiminin maksudu bundan içeru
Senin aşkın beni benden alıptır
Ne şirin dert bu, dermandan içeru
Miskin Yunus, gözü tuş oldu Sana
Kapında bir kuldur, Sultandan içeru

- 18 -

THERE IS AN I IN ME

I have a love for you beyond life within.
I have a way beyond tradition within.

Law and method are for those who take them up.
The fruit of truth transcends beyond and within.

Those who desert religion are blasphemers.
What blasphemy can be beyond faith within.

Do not think I am in me, I am not myself.
There is an I in me past myself within.

My hand reaches not one who takes me from me.
Who can reach a degree past Sultan within.

They say that Solomon converses with birds.
There's a Solomon past Solomon within.

Some have been blessed with manifestation.
There are some whose wish is beyond this, within.

The love of you takes me away from myself.
What lovely trouble 'tis, past the cure within.

Eyes of selfless Yunus surrendered to you,
A servant at your door, past Sultan within.

- 19 -

MEVLAM GÖRELİM NEYLER

Allah diyelim daim
Mevlam görelim neyler
Yolda duralım daim
Mevlam görelim neyler

Sen sanmadığın yerde
Şayet açıla perde
Derman erişe derde
Mevlam görelim neyler

Gündüz olalım saim
Gece olalım kaim
Allah diyelim daim
Mevlam görelim neyler

Netti bu Yunus netti
Bir doğru yola gitti
Bir şeyh eteğin tuttu
Mevlam görelim neyler

- 19 -

SEE WHAT MY LORD MANIFESTS

Allah, Allah let us say,
See what my Lord manifests.
Let's be steadfast on the way,
See what my Lord manifests.

In most unexpected place,
Shall the veil lift off the face,
Let the cure come to the plagues,
See what my Lord manifests.

Daily let us be fasting,
Nightly let us be standing,
God's name let us be chanting,
See what my Lord manifests.

What did this Yunus, what did,
On the right way he is led.
Skirt of attained he held.
See what my lord manifests.

DOST İLE DOST OLMUŞAM

Ben dost ile dost olmuşam
Kimseler dost olmaz bana
Münkirler bakar gülüşür
Selam dahi vermez bana

Ben dost ile dost olayım
Ölmezden evvel öleyim
Canım kurban vereyim
Dünya baki kalmaz bana

Ben aşıkı biçareyim
Baştan ayağa yareyim
Ben bir deli divaneyim
Aklım da yar olmaz bana

Sanurlar ki ben deliyem
Ben dost bağı bülbüliyem
Mevlana'nın kemter kuliyem
Kimse baha saymaz bana

Derviş Yunus nice diyem
Ben bu cihanı terk idem
Yana yana dosta gidem
Perde hicab olmaz bana

I HAVE BECOME A FRIEND WITH FRIEND*

I have become a friend with Friend,
None other could be friend to me.
Deniers look and laugh at me,
They do not even salute me.

Let me become a friend with Friend,
Let me die before my life's end.
Let my life be sacrificial,
World is not immortal to me.

I am but a hopeless lover,
From head to toe I am battered,
I am devastated crazy,
My mind is of no use to me.

They do take me as a madman,
I am a nightingale of Friend,
I am wretched subject of Lord,
No one gives any worth to me.

Dervish Yunus how can I say,
From this world let me go away,
Let me go to Friend burningly,
Curtain is not a veil to me.

*Friend: God within us

- 21 -

LA ILAHE İLLALLAH

Başlayalım söze hoş
Can ü gönül ede cuş
Aşk ile diyelim hoş
La ilahe illallah

Gönülleri şad eder
Kaygudan azad eder
Can mülkün abad eder
La ilahe illallah

Bağlı kapıyı açar
Hakkı batıldan seçer
Gizli sırları açar
La ilahe illallah

Seni sana irgüren
Ölmüş canı dir gören
Bilmezlerin bildiren
La ilahe illallah

Candan teşvişi süren
Kulu Hakka irgüren
Müradına erdiren
La ilahe illallah

Taata yeter seni
Bağışlar suçun Gani
Rahmete iletir seni
La ilahe illallah

- 21 -

LA ILAHE ILLALLAH*

Let us begin pleasantly,
Heart and soul feel joyfully,
With love let us say nicely,
La ilahe illallah.

It fills the heart with gladness,
It sets free from all sadness,
Develops the soul's greatness,
La ilahe illallah.

It opens up the locked door,
Parts superstition from Lord,
It opens up the unknown,
La ilahe illallah.

It directs you towards you,
It restores life to dead soul,
Makes ignorant knowledge full,
La ilahe illallah.

Drives away doubt from the soul,
Directs subject towards Lord,
It reaches one to ones goal,
La ilahe illallah.

It applies one to worship,
Forgives the sins of the rich,
Makes one to blessings reach,
La ilahe illallah.

Can gözün açan budur
Hem arştan gecen budur
Bunu dediren budur
La ilahe illallah

Aşık isen bu ada
Daim getir sen yada
Hak senden olur yana
La ilahe illallah

Evvel narı erişir
Sonra nuru erişir
Hem sururu erişir
La ilahe illallah

Daim eylegil Şükri
Şeytan etmesin mekri
Yunus kalbden et zikri
La ilahe illallah

'Tis one that opens soul's eye,
It passes over the sky,
'Tis one that makes you repeat,
La ilahe illallah.

If you truly love his name,
In memory repeat same,
You always God will claim,
La ilahe illallah.

At first its fire will arrive,
And then its light will arrive,
Also its joy will arrive,
La ilahe illallah.

Always repeat gratitude,
Let not Satan make you mute,
Yunus chant it from the heart,
La ilahe illallah.

*La ilahe illallah: "There is only but one God"

- 22 -

ŞÖYLE HAYRAN EYLE BENİ

Şöyle hayran eyle beni, aşkın adına yanayım
Her ne yana bakar isem gördüğümü sen sanayım

Yedi cehennem dedikleri katlanmaya bir ahıma
Aşkın gönlüm yağmaladı, ben nice katlanayım

Sekiz cennet arzuların yetmiş bin huri gelirse
Aldatamaz bu canımı, bunda nasıl aldanayım

Senin aşkın duydu canım, terkin urdum bu cihanın
Hergiz bilinmez mekanın, seni nerde isteyeyim

Herdem söylenir haberin, hergiz bulunmaz eserin
Götür yüzünden perdeyi, didarına köyüneyim

Yedi deniz geçer isem, yetmiş ırmak içer isem
Susuzluğum kanmaz benim, dost şerbetiyle kanayım

İlm-i hikmet okuyanlar, aşkdan feragahtır bunlar
Mansur oldum asın beni, hep dillerde söyleneyim

- 22 -

FILL ME WITH WORSHIP OF YOU

Fill me with worship of you, let me burn in the fire of love.
Everywhere whomever I see, let me think what I see is you.

What they have called the seven hells, cannot suffer one of my sighs.
Your love has done ran-sacked my heart, and how am I to suffer it.

Even if all the eight heavens, seventy thousand huris* came,
Could not seduce this soul of mine, so how could I be deceived here.

My soul received your lovely scent, I have set out to leave this land.
Not everyone can find your plant, and where am I to look for it.

Every moment is told your news, everyone cannot find your grace,
Remove all the veils of your face, so I can reach beauty of you.

If I cross all seven oceans, if I drink seventy rivers,
My thirst cannot become quenched, let me quench with sherbet of Friend.

The learners of outer science, they are withdrawn from divine love,
Crying "I am Mansur, hang me!", let me be chanted in ballads.

Al götür benden benliği, doldur içime senliği
Gel beni burda öldür, orda varıp ölmeyeyim

Yunus Emre'nin bu sözü, cana doldu evazesi
Kördür münkirlerin gözü, ben nasıl göstereyim

Take away my identity, fill me up inside full of you,
Come to me and make me die here, let me not arrive and die there.

Yunus Emre's are all these words, into his soul filled his loud voice.
The eye of denier is blind, how am I to make him see it.

*huri: according to Islamic belief, huri is a celestial woman that serves one in paradise.

- 23 -

HAKİKATİN MANASIN

Hakikatin manasın şer ile bilmediler
Erenler bu dirliği riyayla dirmediler

Hakikat bir denizdir şeriat onda gemi
Çoklar gemiden çıkıp denize dalmadılar

Dört kitabı şerh eden hakikatte asıydür
Zira tefsir okuyup manasın bilmediler

Şeriat oğlanları bahsedip dava kılar
Hakikat erenleri davaya girmediler

Ödünü sıdır eğer bu yola girdin ise
Ödünü sıdırmayan bu yola gelmediler

Yunus nefsini öldür bu yola geldin ise
Nefsini öldürmeyen bu demi bulmadılar

- 23 -

MEANING OF ACTUAL TRUTH

Meaning of actual truth cannot be known by dogma.
Attained ones this awareness did not get by the falsehood.

The truth is like an ocean, the laws like a ship in it,
Many did not take a dive into the sea from the ship.

One who explains the four books is a rebel to the truth,
Reading interpretation, they have not reached the meaning.

The supporters of the law, they have made a case of it.
Those who have attained the truth did not enter argument.

Take your heart into your hands if you are to enter this,
Those who did not give up fear, did not enter into this.

Yunus destroy your ego if you have come to this road,
Those who did not kill ego, did not attain this degree.

- 24 -

DERVİŞ OLAN KİŞİLER DELİ OLAGAN OLUR

Derviş olan kişiler deli olagan olur
Aşk nedir bilmeyenler ana gülegen olur
Sakın gülme sen ona iyi değildir sana
Kişi neye gülerse başa gelegen olur
Aşık lâmekan olur dünya terkini urur
Dünya terkin uranlar didâr göregen olur
Ah bu aşkın illeri her kime uğrar ise
Derdine sabretmeyen yolda kalagan olur
Bir kişi âşık olsa aşk deryasına dalsa
Ol deryânın dibinden cevher bulagan olur
Derviş Yûnus sen dahi incitme dervişleri
Dervişlerin duâsı makbul olagan olur

- 24 -

CRAZY DERVISH *

Those who become dervishes,
So crazy becominger.
Those who don't know what love is,
Ridicule and laughinger.

Don't you ever laugh at he,
It will not be well for thee,
Whatever one ridicules,
To one's own head cominger.

Lover is non manifest,
Seeks to abandon this world.
Those who would crave abstinence,
Face of God beholdinger.

Oh, the realm of divine love,
If ever calls at one's door,
Those who don't bear with patience,
On the road remaininger.

If one becomes a lover,
And takes a dive at love's ocean,
At the bottom of that sea,
A precious gem findinger.

Ashik Yunus even you,
Do not injure dervishes.
The prayer of dervishes,
God's favored becominger.

*Sometimes Yunus makes up words that are not proper words. Perhaps in this case he is trying to accentuate the craziness of the dervish. I suppose that is called poetic license. A poet can do whatever he wants. It either works or it doesn't.

- 25 -

TEVHİD ETMEK

Tevhid hoşça nesnedir
Gel bile tevhid edelim
Tevhide canlar teşnedir
Gel bile tevhid edelim

Tevhid edenler mestolur
Allah'a erer dost olur
Dirliği hem dürüst olur
Gel bile tevhid edelim

Tevhid eder hep melekler
Döner bu çarhı felekler
Hem huriler hem melekler
Gel bile tevhid edelim

Tevhidi etsin dilimiz
Didarı görsün gözümüz
Dost Muhammed pirimiz
Gel bile tevhid edelim

Tevhid ile biz varalım
Hakk'a yüzümüz sürelim
Yunus bu yolda duralım
Gel bile tevhid edelim

CHANTING LORD'S NAME

Chanting is such a pleasant thing,
Come let us be chanting Lord's name.
Soul is a lover of chanting,
Come let us be chanting Lord's name.

Those who chant will reach ecstasy,
They will reach God and be friendly,
Reach awareness and honesty,
Come let us be chanting Lord's name.

Angels always will be chanting,
Heavens will go on circling,
Celestial women and angels,
Come let us be chanting Lord's name.

Let all our tongues go on chanting,
Let all our eyes see the Lord's face,
With Mohammed as our leader,
Come let us be chanting Lord's name.

With chanting let us all attain,
To the Lord let us rub our face,
Yunus let us wait on this road,
Come let us be chanting Lord's name.

- 26 -

AŞK ETEĞİN TUTMAK GEREK

Aşk eteğin tutmak gerek akıbet zeval olmaya
Aşkdan okuyan bir elif kimseden sual olmaya

Aşk didügin duyarisen aşka candan uyarisen
Aşk yoluna candır feda ona feda mal olmaya

Asılzadeler nişanın eğer bilmek ister isen
Özi oğlan da olursa sözünde vebal olmaya

Ariflerden nişan budur her gönülde hazır ola
Kendini teslim eyleye sözde kıyl-ü kal olmaya

Görmezmisin sen arıyı herbir çiçekten bal eder
Sinek ile pervanenün yuvasında bal olmaya

Dürr ü cevher ister isen ariflere hizmet eyle
Cahil bin söz söyler ise ma'nide miskal olmaya

Miskin Yunus zehr-i katil aşk elinde tiryak olur
İlm ü amel zühd ü taat bes aşksız helal olmaya...

- 26 -

ONE MUST HOLD ON TO SKIRT OF LOVE

If one holds on to skirt of love, for an ending no need will be.
One who reads first letter of love, to ask others no need will be.

If you hear what is known as love, if you are respondent to love,
For sake of love soul sacrifice, wealth sacrifice no need will be.

If you desire to know what is the true sign of nobility,
Even if his essence is man, in all his words no sin will be.

This is the sign of one who knows, who is present in every soul.
He is to surrender himself, in his words no gossip will be.

Do you not see the bee who makes honey out of every flower.
In the nest of the fly or moth, no presence of honey will be.

If you wish pearls or precious gem, pay service to the wise ones.
If ignorant says thousand words, no measure of meaning will be.

Selfless Yunus, fatal poison in love's hands antidote will be.
Works of science, acts of worship, without love no merit will be.

-27-

OL ÇALABUMUN AŞKI

Ol çalabumun aşkı bağrumı baş eyledi
Aldı benim gönlümü sırrımı faş eyledi

Hergiz gitmez gönülden hiç eksik olmaz dilden
Çalab kendi nurunu gözüme tuş eyledi

Can gözü anı gördü dil andan haber verdi
Can içinde oturdu gönlümü arş eyledi

Bir kadeh sundu cana can içdi kana kana
Dolu geldi peymane canı sarhoş eyledi

Esrük oldu canımız dür döker lisanımız
Ol çalabumun aşkı beni sarhoş eyledi

Ben kaçan Derviş olam ta ki ana iş olam
Yüzbin benim gibiyi aşk hırka-puş eyledi

Yunus imdi avunur dostu gördü sevinir
Erenler mahfilinde aşka cünbiş eyledi

-27-

THE LOVE OF MY LORD

The love of that Lord of mine, on my chest a wound he made.
He took my heart, my secret out in the open he made.

He never goes from the heart, he never lacks from the tongue.
Lord, of his very own light, to shine to my eyes he made.

Eye of my soul has seen him, my tongue has mentioned of him.
He placed himself in my soul, and my heart highest he made.

He offered a cup to the soul, the soul drank it to quench.
Full came the cup, and the soul intoxicated he made.

Ecstatic became our soul, pearls are flowing from our words.
The love of that Lord of mine, out of the senses he made.

When I became a dervish and I reached myself to him,
One hundred thousand like me, dressed up with hirka* he made.

Yunus now became consoled, he saw the Lord and rejoiced.
In the gathering of attained, for love song and dance he made.

*hirka: the robe of dervishood

- 28 -

ŞÜKÜR MİNNET OL ALLAHA

Şükür minnet ol Allah'a gönlümüzü şad eyledi
Kafesteki kuşça canım kaygudan azad eyledi

O aşkının bir zerresi bıraktı Mansur gönlüne
Taştı "Ene'l-Hak" diyüben çağırdı feryad eyledi

Güle güle geldi dara eylediler yara yara
Aşık idi ma'şukına hoş dadına dad eyledi

O huyı hoş hem buyı hoş hem güli hem reyhanı hoş
Allah ana dostum didi adın Muhammed eyledi

Yunus senin ma'şukuni sevdi yaratdı ol Gani
Boyu elif kaşları nun gözlerini sad eyledi

- 28 -

THANKS AND GRATITUDE BE TO GOD

Thanks and gratitude be to God, for our hearts joyful he rendered.
My soul like a bird in cage, so free of worry he rendered.

He put a tiny part of his love into the heart of Mansur*.
It filled him so full of joy, he exclaimed "I am God!" he rendered.

Happily he came to be hanged, they wounded him from head to toe.
He was in love with Beloved , he made his justice look pleasant.

One whose nature, and scent, and rose, and his flower was so pleasant,
God claimed him to be his friend, and his name Mohammed he rendered.

Yunus, His Majesty has loved and created your beloved.
His body was "elif", his brow "nun", and his eyes "sad"** he rendered.

*Mansur: a saint that was tortured and hanged by the pious for blasphemy.
**elif, nun, sad: letters from Arabic alphabet.

- 29 -

İŞİTİN EY ULU KİŞİ

İşidün ey ulu kişi size benim haberüm var
Zihi devlet benüm bugün kim şunun gibi yarum var

Yürür isem önümdesin, söyler isem dilümdesin
Oturursam yanumdasın ayruğa ne nazarum var

Ne yüriyemm ne hod aram ne uzak sefere varam
Çünki dostı bunda buldum ayruk neye seferüm var

Irak yola bazirganlar assı itmeye giderler
Çün gevher elümde-durur di ayruk ne bazarum var

Miskin Yunus'un bu canı şol dosta ulaşalıdan
Dem-be-dem artturur aşkı ulu yirden tımarum var

- 29 -

HEAR ME O SUBLIME PEOPLE

Hear me now O sublime people, to bring to you tidings have I.
Lovely kingdom is mine today, ever since such lover have I.

If I walk you are in my heart, If I talk you are on my tongue.
If I sit you are beside me, for all else what desire have I.

Neither do I walk nor I search, nor do I trip to far places.
For I found my Beloved here, for what reason to trip have I.

To far away places merchants go away to make their profit.
For the treasure is in my hands, for what other bargain need I.

Since the soul of selfless Yunus, has arrived at his Beloved,
Day after day adds to his love, from high places healing have I.

SENİ HAK'DAN YIĞAN

Seni Hak'dan yığanı her neyise ver gider
Ne beslersin bu teni sinde kurt kuş yer gider

Ölene bak gözün aç dökülür sakal ve saç
Yılan çılan gelür aç yiyüp içüp sır gider

Bize bizden ulular eğen eyü huylular
Şol eyü amellüler haber söyler dir gider

Kesgil haramdan elün çekgil gaybetten dilün
Azrail el'irmeden bu dükkanı dir gider

Ecel gelir kurur baş tez tükenir uzun yaş
Düpdüz olur dağ ve taş gök dürilür yir gider

Çün can ağdı hazrete yarak it ahirete
Tanla turan taate Tangr'evine ir gider

Miskin Yunus ölicek sini nurla dolucak
İman yoldaş olucak ahirete şir gider

- 30 -

THAT WHICH KEEPS YOU FROM GOD

That which will keep you from God, whatever you have let go.
Why do you feed this body, in grave worms, bugs eat and go.

Open your eyes see the dead, all the hair and beard will shed.
Snake and worm arrive starved, they will eat, drink, fill and go.

Those who are greater than us, those with pleasant natures,
Those who have done such good deeds, leave us their message and go.

Stay your hand from evil deed, stay your tongue from evil speech.
Before angel of death comes, put your house in order and go.

End will come and head will dry, quickly comes to end long life.
Stone and mountain leveled out, sky will roll up and ground will go.

For the soul reaches to Lord, feels the need for after world.
In the dawn stands for worship, to the house of Lord will go.

When selfless Yunus will die, his grave will be full of light.
When faith is his companion, to afterlife bravely will go.

#31

HAK BİR GÖNÜL VİRDİ BANA

Hak bir gönül virdi bana ha dimeden hayran olur
Birdem gelür şadi olur birdem gelür giryan olur

Birdem sanasın kış gibi şol zemheri olmuş gibi
Birdem beşaretden toğar hoş bağ-ıla bustan olur

Birdem gelür söylemez bir sözi şerh eyleyemez
Birdem dilinden dür döker derdlülere derman olur

Birdem çıkar arş üzere birdem iner taht-es-sera
Birdem sanasın katredür birdem taşar Umman olur

Birdem cehaletde kalır kalur hiç nesneyi bilmez olur
Birdem talar hikmetlere Calınus u Lokman olur

Birdem div olur ya peri viraneler olur yiri
Birdem uçar Belkıs ile sultan-ı ins ü can olur

Birdem varur mescidlere yüz sürer anda yirlere
Birdem varur devre girer İncil okur rühban olur

- 31 -

SUCH A HEART LORD HAS GIVEN ME

Such a heart Lord has given me, at once adoring it becomes.
One moment joyful it becomes, one moment sorrowful becomes.

One moment it is winter like, just like a severe winter like,
One moment it's full of good news, a pleasant garden it becomes.

One moment nothing it can say, no explanation it relates.
One moment pearls flow from its tongue, answer to all trouble becomes.

One moment it's on highest sky, one moment it is underground.
One moment you think it's a drop, one moment ocean it becomes.

One moment full of ignorance, oblivious to all becomes,
One moment all full of wisdom, Calinus and Lokman* becomes.

One moment a fairy or gin, its abode an ancient ruin,
One moment it flies with Belkis**, one moment Sultan's soul becomes.

One moment it arrives in mosque, thereupon prostrating itself,
One moment it arrives in church, reads the Bible a priest becomes.

Birdem gelür İsa gibi ölmüşleri diri kılur
Birdem girer Kibr ivine Fir'avn-ıla Haman olur

Birdem döner Cebrail'e rahmet saçar her mahfile
Birdem gelür güm-rah olur miskin Yunus hayran olur

One moment comes just like Jesus, it raises the dead back to life,
One moment enters house of pride, pharaoh and his visier becomes.

One moment turns to Gabriel, scatters blessing to gathering,
One moment it loses its way, poor Yunus adorer becomes

*Calinus: A Greek Scholar; and Lokman: A saint from the era of Job.
**Belkis: An angel from the era of Solomon

- 32 -

SABAHIN SİNLEYE VARDUM

Sabahın sinleye vardum gördüm cümle ölmiş yatar
Her biri-biçare olmış ömrin yavı kılmış yatar

Vardum bunların katına bakdum ecel heybetine
Nice yiğit muradına irememiş ölmiş yatar

Yimiş kurd kuş bunı keler niçelerin bağrın deler
Şol ufacıkta-resteler gül gibice solmuş yatar

Tuzağa düşmiş tenleri Hakk'a ulaşmış canları
Görmez misin sen bunları sıra bize gelmiş yatar

Esilmiş inçi dişleri dökülmüş saru saçları
Kamu bitmiş teşvişleri emr ü nemde ermiş yatar

Gitmiş gözinün karası hiç işi yoktur turası
Kefen bezinin paresi kemiğe sarılmış yatar

Yunus gerçek aşık-ısan mülke suret bezemegil
Mülke suret bezeyenler kara toprak olmış yatar

- 32 -

IN EARLY DAWN I REACHED GRAVEYARD

In early dawn I reached the graveyard, I saw people dead and lying.
Each one having become helpless, having lost his life and lying.

I reached all their different layers, I looked at grandeur of their lives.
Many a hero to their wish, did not reach and died, are lying.

Bugs and worms have eaten them up, many a bosom are pierced up.
Tiny pre puberty children, have faded like roses lying.

Their bodies fallen into trap, their souls having reached to their Lord.
Do you not cast a glance and see, they left our turn to us lying.

Fallen are their pearly white teeth, fallen are their golden blonde hair.
Came to end their earthly struggles, they have reached God's will and lying.

Gone are the colour of their eyes, non-existent light of their life.
Pieces of cloth of their shroud, wrapped around their bones and lying.
Yunus if you are true lover, do not turn your face towards wealth.
Those who turned their faces to wealth, have become dark earth and lying.

- 33 -

AŞIK OLANLARIN İŞİ...

Hocam aşık olanların işi ah-ile zar olur
Hasretinden o ma'şukun, gözün yaşı Pınar olur

Dünü günü kılar zarı, ya'ni görmek diler yârı
İşitmezler bu haberi aşksızlar bi-haber olur

Aşık isen didarına, koyma bu günü yarına
Girenler aşk bazarına, kendisinden bize olur

Terk eyle sen benliğini, onun aşkında kıl taleb
Bu aşk içinde olanın, kan bahası didar olur

Hani gerçek aşık hani, gelin isteyelim onu
Biçare Yunus'un canı, dost yoluna isar olur

- 33 -

THE LOT OF THOSE WHO ARE LOVERS

O teacher, those who are lovers, their lot full of hardship becomes.
From yearning for the beloved, tears of their eyes fountain becomes.

Day in day out remains weeping, for he wants to see beloved.
They do not receive word of this, loveless oblivious becomes.

If you are in love with beauty, don't leave today to tomorrow.
One who enters market of love, weary of himself he becomes.

Leave individuality, make his love your only desire.
For the one who is in this love, gain of his loss beauty becomes.

Where is genuine lover where, come let us make request of him.
The life of poor wretched Yunus, for sake of Friend offered becomes.

- 34 -

YİNE SEYR EYLEDİ GÖNLÜM

Yİne seyr eyledi gönlüm dostun cemalin arzular
Hicre katlanamaz gönül dostun cemalin arzular

Her kim uğrarsa bu derde o bulur himmeti erde
Açılıviricek perde dostun cemalin arzular

Kim ki gerçek mürid ola bil bağlayup gelsün yola
Şol yürekteki derd ola dostun cemalin arzular

Dostum beni deli kıldı aklımı fikrimi aldı
Hayali gözümde kaldı dostun cemalin arzular

Evvel dirdi gönlüm bana atlar tonlar gerek bana
Mevlam bir derd verdi bana dostun cemalin arzular

Yunus'un sözü içince iniler canın verince
Ta ölüp sine girince dostun cemalin arzular

- 34 -

MY HEART HAS SEEN IT AGAIN

My heart has seen it once again, the beauty of Lord it desires.
Heart suffers not separation, the beauty of Lord it desires.

Whoever meets up with this fate, receives help from the attained ones.
Suddenly will lift up the veil, the beauty of Lord he desires.

Whoever is true disciple, let him get tied up with this way.
Dilemma of his heart becomes, the beauty of Lord he desires.

My Beloved rendered me mad, took my mind away from myself.
His vision remained in my eye, the beauty of Lord it desires.

Before my heart used to tell me, horses and clothes I need.
My Lord gave me such a dilemma, the beauty of Lord it desires.

When words of Yunus come to end, he whimpers when he gives his soul.
Till he dies and enters his grave, the beauty of Lord he desires.

- 35 -

MA'Nİ EVİNE DALDIK

Ma'ni evine daldik vücûdı seyran kılduk
İki cihan seyrini cümle vücudda bulduk

Bu çizginen gökleri taht-es-sera yirleri
Yetmiş bin hicabları cümle vücudda bulduk

Yedi yer yedi gökü dağları denizleri
Uçmağ-ıla tamuyı cümle vücudda bulduk

Gece ile gündüzü gökte yedi yıldızı
Lehde yazılı sözü cümle vücudda bulduk

Musi ağduğı Tur'ı Kuds-de Beyt-ül-ma'muri
İsrafil urduğ suri cümle vücudda bulduk

Tevrat ile İncil'i Kuran ile Zebur'ı
Bunlardağı beyanı cümle vücudda bulduk

Yunus'un sözleri hak, cümlemiz didük saddak
Kanda istersen anda Hak cümle vücudda bulduk

- 35 -

TO HOUSE OF MEANING WE DOVE

To house of meaning we dove, the body we have observed.
Site of both universes, all in the body we found.

All of these revolving skies, the earth and the underground,
All seventy thousand veils, all in the body we found.

Seven earth and seven skies, the mountains and all the seas,
The hell and the paradise, all in the body we found.

Both of the day and the night, all of the stars in the sky,
The words written on the scrolls, all in the body we found.

The Mount Sinai Moses climbed, house of angels in the sky,
The pipe that Israfil* blows, all in the body we found.

The Torah and the Bible, the Koran and the Zebur**.
And the commandments in these, all in the body we found.

The words of Yunus are right, with this all of us comply,
Where you wish the Lord is there, all in the body we found.

*   Israfil: the angel that brings in the end of world.
** Zebur: the book of King David.

- 36 -

EYLE BİZİ

İlahi cennet evine
Girenlerden eyle bizi
Yarın anda cemalini
Görenlerden eyle bizi

Mahşerde halk ola hayran
Çok yürekler ola büryan
Arşın gölgesinde seyran
Edenlerden eyle bizi

Ya hayy ü ya kayyum samed
İhsanına yoktur aded
Firdevs bahçesinde ebed
Kalanlardan eyle bizi

Bu dünyanın cefası çok
Kimi aç gezer kimi tok
Şol mizanda sevabı çok
Gelenlerden eyle bizi

Bakma dünyanın varına
Düşüp daim Hak yoluna
Beratını sağ eline
Alanlardan eyle bizi

Mü'minlere rahmet ola
Münafıklar mahrum kala
Yunus gider doğru yola
Gidenlerden eyle bizi

- 36 -

RENDER US

Into divine house of heaven,
Those who will enter, render us.
Tomorrow your beautiful face,
Those who get to see, render us.

Judgement day people adoring,
Many hearts in their nakedness,
Under shade of heaven's ceiling,
Those who will behold, render us.

Among those who will hear and speak,
To your gifts there is no limit,
In heaven's garden forever,
Those who will remain, render us.

Suffering of world is many,
Some hungry some full bellied,
In the judgement of afterlife,
With many merits, render us.

Do not look at wealth of this world,
Be always on the way to Lord,
Their acquittal in their right hand,
Those who have obtained, render us.

May the believers get God's grace,
May deniers get deprived face,
Yunus goes on the righteous ways,
Among those who go, render us.

ALLAH DEYU DEYU

Şu Cennetin ırmakları
Akar Allah deyu deyu
Hem içinde Burak'ları
Otlar Allah deyu deyu

Salınır Tuba dalları
Taze açılır gülleri
Her dalında bülbülleri
Öter Allah deyu deyu

Kimi yiyip kimi içer
Etrafa gevherler saçar
İdris Nebi hülle biçer
Diker Allah deyu deyu

Ol Allahın melekleri
Daim tesbihte dilleri
Cennet bağı çiçekleri
Kokar Allah deyu deyu

Yunus eydür ben de varsam
Hakk'ın cemalini görsem
Nurdan Burak'lara binsem
Gezsem Allah deyu deyu

CHANTING ALLAH ALLAH*

Those rivers of the paradise,
They flow chanting Allah Allah.
The Buraks** inside the heavens,
They graze chanting Allah Allah.

Swinging branches of the Tuba***
Open fresh blossoming roses.
With nightingales on every branch,
They sing chanting Allah Allah.

Some are eating, some are drinking,
Some precious gems scattering,
Idris Nebi**** is cloth cutting,
Sewing, chanting Allah Allah.

Those celestial angels of God,
With all their tongues on rosary,
Vineyard flowers of heaven,
They smell chanting Allah Allah.

Yunus says let me too arrive,
Let me look upon God's delight.
Ride the Buraks made of God's light,
Tripping, chanting Allah Allah.

*Allah: God
** Burak: A celestial horse sent by God for Mohammed to ascend to heaven.
*** Tuba: Name given to a tree in paradise
****Idris Nebi: According to Islam belief he was the first prophet to sew clothes.

#38

CANUM BEN ANDAN

Canum ben andan bunda ezeli aşık geldüm
Aşkı kulavuz tutup ol yola düşüp geldüm

Değülem kal ü kiylden ya yitmiş iki dilden
Yad yok bana bu ilde anda bilişüp geldüm

Geçdüm hod-bin ilinden el çekdüm dükeliden
Ol ikilik babından birliğe bitüp geldüm

Dört kişidir yoldaşum vefadar u raz-daşum
Üçile hoştur başum birine buşup geldüm

Ol dördün birisi can biri din biri iman
Birin nefsümdür düşman anda savaşup geldüm

Bir kılı kırk yardılar birin yol gösterdiler
Bu mülke gönderdiler ol yola düşüp geldüm

Aşk şerbetinden içdüm on sekiz ırmak geçdüm
Denizler bendin deşdüm ummandan taşup geldüm

Ben andan güldüm bunda girü varuram anda
Ben anda varasumı anda tanışup geldüm

Azrail ne kişidür kasd idesi canuma
Ben emanet ıssı-yla anda bitrişüp geldüm

İmdi Yunus'a ne gam aşık melamet bed-nam
Küfrüm imana şol dem anda degşürüp geldüm

- 38 -

MY SOUL FROM THERE

O my soul from there to here, eternal lover I've come.
Holding love as my guidance, falling on that road I've come.

I'm not the sort that gossips, or who speaks seventy-two tongues.
None is stranger to me here, there knowing all I have come.
I passed from realm of conceit, I withdrew my hand from all.
From door of duality, to the oneness I have come.
And my companions are four, all my faithful confidants.
I am on good terms with three, with one angry I've become.
Of the four, one is my soul, one religion other faith,
One is my ego, my foe, with him I've made war I've come.
They sliced hair into forty, they pointed one as the way.
They sent me to this estate, falling on that road I've come.

I've drunk the nectar of love, eighteen rivers I have passed.
Demolished bed of oceans, overflowing I have come.

From there I have come to here, again will I return there,
My returning back to there, having pre arranged I've come.

What person is Lucifer, that he should attempt my life.
With a life that has been loaned, I've agreed to there and I've come.

What grief is it Yunus, that lover falls to ill fame.
My blasphemy equals faith, there I've exchanged and I've come.

- 39 -

HABER EYLEN AŞIKLARA

Haber eylen aşıklara aşka gönül veren benem
Aşk bahrısı olubanı denizlere talan benem

Yir gök tolu bu aşk-durur aşkdan yiğreği yok-durur
Aşka baha kim yitüre ma'den-i kan olan benem

Deniz yüzinden su alup Sünni-virürem göklere
Bulut-layın seyran idüp arşa yakın varan benem

Yıldırım olup şakıyan gökde melaik dokuyan
Bulutlara hüküm süren yağmur olup yağan benem

Gördüm göğün meleklerin her biri bir işde-y-miş
Hak Çalabun zikrin ider İncil benem Kur'an benem

Gördüm diyen değül gören bildim diyen değül bilen
Bilen oldur gösteren ol aşka yesir olan benem

Kalem çalınıcak görgil haber böyle-durur bilgil
Kalu bela kelccisin bunda haber viren benem

Delü oldum adım Yunus aşk oldu bana kulavuz
Hazrete değin yalunuz yüz sürüyi varan benem

- 39 -

SEND MESSAGE TO LOVERS

Send the message to the lovers, one who gives heart to love I
am.
Becoming a mallard of love, one who dives into sea I am.

Earth and sky are full of this love, better than love nothing there
is.
Who makes comparison to love, like the mineral spring I
am.

Taking water from the ocean, I send it up to the heavens.
Like clouds casting a look downwards, one who approaches sky
I am.

Becoming lightning and lighting, angels to each other weaving.
Having command over the clouds, becoming rain falling I
am.

I saw the angels in the sky, each one busy with a duty,
Repeating praises to the Lord, Bible I am Koran I am.

The one who says I saw did not, the one who says I know does not.
Knower is he, shower is he, the one who's slave to love I
am.

What the pen has written see it, like this the news will be

know it.
The meaning of Kalu Bela*, the one who offers here I am.

I am mad my name is Yunus, and love has become my guidance.
To Lord's presence all by myself, one who arrives face down I am.

*Kalu Bela: a verse from the Koran

- 40 -

KİM DERVİŞLİK İSTER İSE

Kim dervişlik ister-ise diyem ona n'itmek gerek
Şerbeti elinden koyup ağuyı nuş itmek gerek

Gelmek gerek terbiyete cümle bildiklerin koya
Mürebbisi ne dir-ise bes ol anı dutmak gerek

Tuta sabr u kanaati tahammül eyleye katı
Terk eyleye suretüni bildiğin unutmak gerek

Dünyadan gönlünü çeke eli-y-ile arpa eke
Unına yarı kül kata güneşde kurutmak gerek

Diyem ona nice ide nefsi dileğin bu yolda
Kaçan kim iftar eyleye üç günde bir itmek gerek

Böyledir derviş dirliği koya cümle ayyarlığı
Andan bulisar erlüği kahırlar çok yutmak gerek

Bakma dünya sevüsine aldanma halk gövüsine
Dönüp didar arzusına ol Hakk'a yüz tutmak gerek

Yunus imdi nedir dersin ya kimin kaydını yersin
Bir kişi bu sözü desin ona gücü yetmek gerek

- 40 -

WHOEVER DESIRES DERVISHOOD

Whoever desires dervishood, let me tell him what is needed.
Giving up sherbet from one's hand, to drink the poison is needed.

One needs to come to be re-trained, one has to give up all retained.
Whatever one's teacher commands, to yield and obey is needed.

Keep patience, determination, and to endure and suffer much,
To abandon one's demeanor, to forget all one knows is needed.

To withdraw one's heart from the world, to plant barley with one's own hand.
To add ashes to its flour, to dry it in the sun's needed.

Let me tell how he should react to the desire of his ego.
How often is he to partake, eat once every three days' needed.

This is lifestyle of the dervish, to abandon all enmity.
From that he derives attainment, to suffer much grief is needed.

Do not look at love of the world, or reliance of the people.
To turn to desire of beauty, to turn face to God is needed.

Yunus, what word are you saying, of whom are you making concern.
Whoever is stating this word, to live up to it is needed.

- 41 -

YÜRÜ EY GÖNÜL

Yürü ey gönül sen bir zaman asude fariğ koş yürü
Korkma kayurma kimseden gussa vü gamdan boş yürü

Hakikate bakar isen nefsün sana düşman yiter
Var imdi ol nefsün ile urış savaş tokış yürü

Nefsdür eri yolda koyan yolda kalır nefse uyan
Ne işin var kimseyile nefsüne kakı buş yürü

Diler-isen bu dünyanın şerrinden olasın emin
Terk eyle bu kibr u kini hırkaya gir derviş yürü

İster-isen bu dünyada ebedi sarhoş olasın
Aşk kadehin dolu getür yıl on-iki ay sarhoş yürü

Kimse bağına girmegil kimse gülini dirmegil
Var kendi ma'şukun ile bağçede ol alış yürü

Gönüller'de iğ olmagıl mahfillerde çiğ olmagıl
Çiğ nesnenün ne dadı var gel aşk odına biş yürü

Yunus imdi hoş söylersin dinleyene şerh eylersin
Halka nasihat satınca er ol yolınca koş yürü

- 41 -

WALK O HEART

Oh heart walk for some time in peace, then leave comfort and run and walk.
Fear not and withdraw from no one, free of fear anxiety walk.

If you look at reality, your ego is a foe to you.
Go ahead now reach the ego, fight, make battle with it and walk.

It is ego that gets you stuck, one who suits the ego is stuck.
Break all your ties with everyone, scold your ego be free and walk.

If you wish to attain freedom, from all of the laws of this world,
Abandon all pride and all hate, put on cloak of dervishood walk.

If you desire to be ever-intoxicated in this world,
Keep your cup of love full to brim, twelve months a year be drunk and walk.

Enter into no one's garden, gather no one else's roses.
Arrive now with your beloved, in the garden exchange and walk.

Do not be a fog in the heart, do not be raw at gathering.
Something raw does not have flavour, cook in the fire of love and walk.

Yunus, now you tell pleasantly, you explain to one who

listens.
Giving advice to the people, reach along that road, run and walk.

- 42 -

EYA GÖNÜL AÇGIL GÖZÜN

Eya gönül açgıl gözün fikrin yavlak uzatmagil
Bakgil kendi dirliğüne kimse aybın gözetmegil

Şöyle dirilgil halk-ıla öleceğiz söyleşeler
Bakı dirlik budur canum yavuz ad-ıla gitmegil

Diler-isen bu dünyayı ahirete degşüresin
Dün ü gün kılgıl taatı ayak uzatıp yatmagil

Gördün ki bir derviş gelir yüz ur anun kademine
Senden şey'ullah idicek kaşın karağın çatmagil

Söylediğin keleciyi işittiğin gibi söyle
Kendüzünden zireklenip bir kaç söz dahi katmagil

Dünya çerb ü şirin-durur adem gerekir yiyesi
Kem nesneye tama edip kösüp kömürüp yutmagil

Nefse uyup beş parmağın iltme ağzına
Kes birisin ver miskine gerek ola unutmagil

Yunus kim öldürür seni veren alır gene canı
Yarın göresin sen anı er nazarından gitmegil

- 42 -

OH HEART OPEN YOUR EYES

Oh my heart, do open your eyes, do not harp on your ideas.
Take a look at your own lifestyle, others' shame do not be watching.

Maintain well-being with people, it is said that we are to die.
This is real immortality, with bad name do not be going.

If you are desiring this world, you'll exchange it with after world.
Day in day out perform worship, do not stretch out and be sleeping.

When you see a dervish coming, turn your face to his well being.
When he'll make a request of you, your eyebrows do not be frowning.

Words of meaning that you repeat, recite them as you have heard them.
Getting understanding from him, your own words do not be adding.

The world appears so appeasing, son of man needs to consume it.
Having desire for something bad, with greed do not be devouring.

Going along with your ego, push not five fingers to your mouth.
Cut one off and give to needy, mind you do not be forgetting.

Yunus, who is it that slays you, one who gives you life takes it back.
Tomorrow you get to see him, from glance of saints don't be running.

- 43-

BU DÜNYAYA GELEN KİŞİ

Bu dünyaya gelen kişi ahır yine gitse gerek
Misafirdir vatanına bir gün sefer etse gerek

Va'de kıldık ol dost-ıla biz bu cihana gelmedin
Pes ne kadar eğlenevüz ol va'demüz yitse gerek

Biz de varavuz ol ile kaçan ki va'demüz gele
Kişi varacağı yere gönlünü berkitse gerek

Gönlü nice berkitmeye dost iline giden yola
Aşık kişiler canını bu yola harc itse gerek

Can neye ulaşır-ısa akıl da ona harc olur
Gönül neyi sever ise dil onu şerh itse gerek

Acep midir aşık kişi ma'şukını zikr ederse
Aşk başından aşıcağız gönlünü zar itse gerek

Yunus imdi sever-isen ondan haber vergiler bize
Aşkın oldur nişanı ma'şukın eyitse gerek

- 43 -

ONE WHO HAS COME TO THIS WORLD

The one who has come to this world, in the end to leave it he must.
He is just a guest in his land, one day to make journey he must.

We have made a term with that friend, before we have come to this land.
No matter how much entertained, our term to come to end it must.

And we will too arrive at it, whenever our term has matured.
Person to his destination, to re-enforce his heart he must.

The heart is made to be strengthened, on the road that goes to Friend's realm.
The ones who are lovers, their soul, on this road to spend it they must.

Whatever the soul reaches for, the mind too will be spent at it.
Whatever the heart's in love with, the tongue to interpret it must.

And is it any wonder that the lover should praise beloved.
With love exceeding over head, to rant and rave his heart he must.

Yunus if you are true lover, bestow to us tidings of him.
The sign of true lover is that to speak of Beloved he must.

- 44 -

BUNDA BENİM KARARIM YOK

Benim bunda kararım yok ben gine gitmeye geldim
Bazirganam metaum çok alana satmağa geldim

Ben gelmedim da'vi-y-içün benüm işüm sevi-y-içün
Dostun evi gönüllerdür gönüller yapmağa geldim

Dost esrüği delüliğün aşıklar bilir neliğün
Degyürüben ikiliğün birliğe yetmeğe geldim

O padişah ben kuluyam dost bahçesi bülbüliyem
Ol hocamın bahçesine şad olup ötmeye geldim

Bunda bilişmeyen canlar anda bilişemez anlar
Bilişüben dost-ıla ben halüm arz etmeye geldim

Yunus eydür aşık oldum ma'şuka derdinden öldüm
Gerçek erün kapısında ömrüm harc etmeye geldim

- 44 -

I HAVE NO INTENT OF STAYING HERE

I've no intent of staying here, only to return I have come.
I'm a merchant, my goods many, to sell to the buyers I've come.

I have not come for a quarrel, my business is only with love.
Residence of Friend are the hearts, to enter the hearts I have come.

Madness of ecstasy of Friend, only lovers would know what is.
Transcending from duality, to arrive at oneness I've come.

Subject of that Sultan I am, his garden's nightingale I am.
In the garden of my teacher, to be joyful and sing I've come.

The souls that do not know him here, they will not get to know him there.
Getting acquainted with Friend, to plead my case with him I've come.

Yunus says I've become lover, for sake of beloved I died.
At the door of the true attained, to spend all my life I have come.

- 45 -
İLİM İLİM BİLMEKTİR...

İlim ilim bilmektir
İlim kendin bilmektir
Sen kendini bilmezsin
Ya nice okumaktır

Okumadan ma'na ne
Kişi Hakk'kı bilmektir
Çün okudun bilmezsin
Ha bir kuru emektir

Okudum bildim deme
Çok taat kıldım deme
Eri Hak bilmez isen
Abes yire yilmekdir

Dört kitabın ma'nası
Bellidir bir elifde
Sen elifi bilmezsin
Bu nice okumakdır

Yirmi dokuz hece
Okusan ucdan uca
Sen elif dersin hoca
Ma'nası ne demekdir

Yunus Emre'dir hoca
Gerekse var bin hacca
Hepisinden eyüce
Bir gönüle girmekdir

- 45 -

SCIENCE IS HAVING KNOWLEDGE

Science is having knowledge,
Knowledge is knowing yourself.
If you do not know yourself,
All your reading is for naught.

What is purpose of reading,
For a person to know God.
If you know not by reading,
All your toil is for nothing.

Say not you have read and know,
Say not you have paid worship,
If you are not knowing God,
You are running after void.

The meaning of the four books
Is known in the first letter.
If you do not know the first,
What sort of reading is that.

All of twenty-nine letters,
If you read from end to end,
You say elif* to teacher,
What is the meaning of it.

Yunus Emre says hodja**,
Do thousand pilgrimages.
Much better than all of that
Is to enter someone's heart.

*elif: first letter of Arabic alphabet
** hodja: Moslem priest

İSTEDİĞİMİ BULDUM

İstediğimi buldum eşkere can içinde
Taşra isteyen kendi kendi nihan içinde

Kadimdir hiç ırılmaz onsuz kimse dirilmez
Adım adım yer ölçer hükmü revan içinde

Tutun diye çağırır hırsız diye bağırır
Bu ne acayip hırsız bu çağıran içinde

Siyaset meydanında galebeden bakan ol
Siyaset kendi olmuş girmiş meydan içinde

Tartmış kudret kılıcın çalmış nefsin boynını
Nefsini depelemiş elleri kan içinde

Bu tılsımı bağlayan cümle dilde söyleyen
Yere göğe sığmayan gelmiş cihan içinde

Uğrı olmuş uğrılar geri kendisi çakar
Şahne kendisi olmuş kendi zindan içinde

Türlü türlü imaret köşk ü saray yapan ol
Kara nikab tutunmuş girmiş külhan içinde

Başdan ayağa değin Hakdur ki seni tutmuş
Hak'dan ayrı ne vardır kalma güman içinde

I FOUND WHAT I HAD DESIRED

I found what I had desired, plainly in the soul within.
Wants to be revealed himself, with himself hidden within.

Without beginning, so near, without him no one can be,
Step by step he measures ground, his rule in the soul within.

Saying "catch him" he calls out, the burglar he calls out loud.
What manner burglar is it, inside the caller within.

On the field of punishment, he looks from within the crowd.
He's become the punishment, has entered the field within.

He has drawn the sword of might, has struck upon ego's neck.
He has trampled his ego, with his hands in blood within.

He's become ill he whimpers, sound of Koran he listens.
He's the one who reads Koran, he's inside Koran within.

The one who ties knot of spell, one who speaks on every tounge,
Uncontained by sky or ground, has come in the world within.

He has become thief he steals, after himself he chases,
He has become guard himself, himself in dungeon within.

Biriysen birliğe gel ikiyi bırak elden
Bütün ma'na bulasın sıdk u iman içinde

Girdim gönül şehrine daldım onun bahrına
Aşkile gideriken iz buldum can içinde

Bu izimi izledim sağım solum gözledim
Çok acayipler gördüm yoktur cihan içinde

Yunus senin sözlerin ma'nadır bilenlere
Söyleniser sözlerin devr-i zaman içinde

Variety of buildings, builder of palace is he,
Embarrassed by poverty, he's in a shelter within.

All the way from head to toe, it is the Lord holding you
What is there apart from Lord, do not be in doubt within.

If you're one, come to oneness, give up on duality,
Discover all the meaning, inside the true faith within.

I entered city of heart, I dove into its ocean.
While I was going with love, I found tracks in soul within.

And I have followed these tracks, I have glanced to left and right,
I saw many strange things, not to be found in world within.

These words of Yunus are filled, with meaning to those who know.
Let them repeat all his words, in ages to come within

İSTER İDİM ALLAHI

İster idim Allahı
Bulduk ise ne oldu
Ağlar idik dün ü gün
Güldük ise ne oldu

Erenler meclisinde
Biz bir pare gül idik
Açıldık ele geldik
Solduk ise ne oldu

Danişmendle alimin
Medresede bulduğun
Biz harabat içinde
Bulduk ise ne oldu

Erenler meydanında
Yükü yüklenir duyduk
Padişah çevkanında
Kaldık ise ne oldu

İşit Yunus'u işit
O yine derviş oldu
Erenler ma'nisine
Daldık ise ne oldu

I USED TO BE WANTING GOD

I used to be wanting God,
If I found him, what of it.
I used to weep day and night,
I found laughter, what of it.

In the council of attained,
I was a bunch of roses.
I bloomed and came into hand,
If I wilted, what of it.

What the learned men have found
In schools of theology,
I have found in the tavern,
If I found it, what of it.

In the field of the attained,
I used to be loading up.
In the court of the Sultan,
If I remained, what of it.

Hear ye, Yunus here and now,
He became dervish again.
To the meaning of attained,
If I have dived, what of it.

AŞKIN VER ŞEVKİN VER

Yarabbi dilerim
Aşkın ver şevkin ver
Fazlından umarım
Aşkın ver şevkin ver

Mest eyle sen beni
Bilmeyim ben seni
Ta bula can seni
Aşkın ver şevkin ver

Yolunda aşıklar
Derdinle yanıklar
Canlardan geçtiler
Aşkın ver şevkin ver

Kalbini pak eyle
Masiva hubbünü sil
Hubbünü ata kıl
Aşkın ver şevkin ver

Derviş Yunus Kuluna
Nazar eyle haline
İrgüresin vaslına
Aşkın ver şevkin ver

- 48 -

GIVE LOVE AND EAGERNESS

My Lord I beseech thee,
Give love and eagerness.
Exceedingly I hope,
Give love and eagerness.

Lead me to ecstasy,
Let me be lost in thee,
Till my soul is made free,
Give love and eagerness.

On your way are lovers,
Burning with your worries,
Have given up their lives,
Give love and eagerness.

Render all our hearts pure,
Wipe ungodly nature,
Cast away bad habit,
Give love and eagerness.

To your Yunus subject
Cast your glance to his state.
Lead him to attainment,
Give love and eagerness.

BU DÜNYANIN MİSALİ

Bu dünyanın misali
Muazzam şehre benzer
Veli bizim ömrümüz
Biz tez bazare benzer

Her kim bu şehre gelse
Bir lahza bazar kılsa
Dönüp yine gitmesi
Gelmez sefere benzer

Bu şehrin hayalleri
Türlü türlü halleri
Aldanmış gaafilleri
Cazı ve ayara benzer

Bu şehirde çoktur hayal
Vasfında yoktur mecal
Ol hayale aldananlar
Sıcakta kara benzer

Bu şehrin Sultanı var
Kamuya ihsanı var
Sultan ile birleşen
Yokiken vara benzer

Bu miskin Yunus Derviş
Sararmış harab olmuş
Veli aşkın deminde
Evvel-bahara benze

- 49-

THE EXAMPLE OF THIS WORLD

The example of this world
A great city resembles.
On the other hand our lives
A quick market resembles.

Whoever comes to this city
Sets up shop for a moment.
His turning and returning
One way trip it resembles.

Of this city's illusions,
So many disillusions,
All its deceived ignorant,
Fraud and con it resembles.

This city's dreams are many.
There's no strength in its essence.
One who's taken by those dreams,
Snow in the heat resembles.

This city a sultan has,
To the people gifts he has,
One who unites with sultan,
Exist from naught resembles.

This selfless humble Yunus
Is faded devastated.
However on stage of love
A fresh spring he resembles.

- 50 -

NİÇİN AĞLARSIN BÜLBÜL

Sen bunda garip mi geldin
Niçin ağlarsın bülbül hey
Yârinden ayrı mı düştün
Niçin ağlarsın bülbül hey

Hey ne yavuz inilersin
Benim derdim yenilersin
Dostu görmek mi dilersin
Niçin ağlarsın bülbül hey

Kanadın açabilirsin
Açuban uçabilirsin
Hicablar geçebilirsin
Niçin ağlarsın bülbül hey

Kal'a şehrin mi yıkıldı
Ya namı arın mı kaldı
Gurbette yarın mı kaldı
Niçin ağlarsın bülbül hey

Gülistanlık yayılırsın
Benim derdim yenilersin
Yunus gibi inilersin
Niçin ağlarsın bülbül hey

- 50 -

WHY DO YOU WEEP O NIGHTINGALE

Did you arrive a stranger here,
Why do you weep O nightingale.
Have you been parted from your love,
Why do you weep O nightingale.

So heart breakingly you whimper,
You rekindle all my trouble,
Do you desire to see the Lord,
Why do you weep O nightingale.

You are able to open wings,
You can open them up and fly,
You can transcend all kinds of veils,
Why do you weep O nightingale.

Has your city been demolished,
Has your reputation been shamed,
Is your lover in foreign land,
Why do you weep O nightingale.

You spread over land of roses,
You rekindle all my troubles,
You do whimper just like Yunus,
Why do you weep O nightingale.

İNCİTME DERVİŞLERİ

Dinin imanın var ise
Hor görme gel dervişleri
Cümle alem müştakdurur
Görmekliğe dervişleri

Ay ve güneş maşuk durur
Dervişlerin sohbetine
Feriştehler teşbih okur
Zikrederler dervişleri

Ol Muhammedil Mustafa
Derviş idi gönlü safa
İster isen ondan vefa
İncitme gel dervişleri

İncidesin ah edeler
Gözsüz olasın yedekler
Aslın kökün kurudalar
İncidirsen dervişleri

Derviş oku uzak atar
Deymeden hiç cana batar
Gafil olma yırtar tutar
Hor görme gel dervişleri

Dört kitabın manasını
Günde bin kez okur isen
Yarın piranı görmezsin
Sevmez isen dervişleri

- 51 -

DO NOT INJURE DERVISHES

If you have religion and faith,
Do not look down on dervishes.
All creation is desirous,
To be seeing the dervishes.

Moon and sun in admiration,
Of the sohbet* of dervishes,
The angels with their rosary,
Are chanting of the dervishes.

That Mohammedil Mustafa,
A true dervish was his clean heart,
If you desire his faithfulness,
Do not injure the dervishes.

If you injure them they will sigh,
And they will curse you to be blind,
And your foundation they will dry,
If you injure the dervishes.

Arrow of the dervish shoots far,
Without touching it pierces heart,
Don't be fool, it will tear apart,
Do not look down on dervishes.

The meaning of all the four books,
If you read thousand times a day,
Tomorrow you will not attain,
If you do not love dervishes.

Bu dervişler bir kuşdürür
Allah ile bilişdürür
Bilmeyene bir düşdürür
Kande göre dervişleri

Derdli kişi bilir bizi
Daim sorar halimizi
Kördür münkirlerin gözü
Görmeyiser dervişleri

Yunus eydür bu aşk geldi
Ölmüş canım diri kıldı
Senlik benlik dilde kaldı
Göreceğiz dervişleri

These dervishes are like a bird,
They are uniting with the Lord,
To those who don't know it's a dream,
That they will see the dervishes.

Troubled people know of our lot,
They constantly ask of our state,
Blind is the eye of denier,
They do not see the dervishes.

Yunus says this love did arrive,
It has made alive the dead life,
Duality became just words,
We will get to see dervishes.

*spiritual discourse, sermon

-52-

DAĞLAR İLE TAŞLAR İLE

Dağlar ile, taşlar ile çağırayım Mevlam seni
Seherlerde kuşlar ile, çağırayım Mevlam seni

Sular dibinde mahi ile, sahralarda ahu ile
Abdal olup "Ya Hu" ile, çağırayım Mevlam seni

Gök yüzünde İsa ile, Tur dağında Musa ile
Elimde asa ile, çağırayım Mevlam seni

Derdi öküş Eyyup ile, gözü yaşlı Yakup ile
Ol Muhemmed mahbub ile çağırayım Mevlam seni

Hamd ü şükrullah ile, vasf-ı Kulhüvallah ile
Daima zikrullah ile, çağırayım Mevlam seni

Bilmişim dünya halini, terk ettim kıyl ü kalini
Baş açık ayak yalın, çağırayım Mevlam seni

- 52-

MY SWEET LORD

With the boulders and the mountain,
Let me call thy name my sweet Lord.
With all the birds in early dawn,
Let me call thy name my sweet Lord.

With all the fish deep in the sea,
With the gazelle running so free,
With sound of HU in ecstasy,
Let me call thy name my sweet Lord.

In the heavens with sweet Jesus,
On the mountain with dear Moses,
Holding shepherd's staff in his hands,
Let me call thy name my sweet Lord.

With Job and his heart so troubled,
And with Jacob, tears in his eyes,
With Mohammed, thy beloved,
Let me call thy name my sweet Lord.

With gratitude and thankfulness,
With wisdom of holy verses,
With constant praise of thy greatness,
Let me call thy name my sweet Lord.

I've known the ways of earthly fare,
Abandoned all gossip and care,
With open head and my feet bare,
Let me call thy name my sweet Lord.

Yunus okur diller ile, ol kumru bülbüller ile
Hakkı seven kullar ile, çağırayım Mevlam seni

Yunus recites with rhyming tongue,
With every nightingale and dove,
With God's loving, faithful people,
Let me call thy name my sweet Lord

- 53 -

BİR ŞAHA KUL OLMAK GEREK

Bir şaha kul olmak gerek
Hergiz ma'zul olmaz ola
Bir eşik yaslanmak gerek
Kimse elden almaz ola

Bir kuş olup uçmak gerek
Bir kenara geçmek gerek
Bir şerbetten içmek gerek
İçenler ayılmaz ola

Çevik Bahri olmak gerek
Bir denize dalmak gerek
Bir cevher çıkarmak gerek
Hiç sarraflar bilmez ola

Bir bahçeye girmek gerek
Hoş teferrüç kılmak gerek
Bir gülü koklamak gerek
Herkes ol gül Solmaz ola

Kişi aşık olmak gerek
Ma'şukayı bulmak gerek
Aşk adına yanmak gerek
Ayruk oda yanmaz ola

Yunus imdi var dek otur
Yüzünü hazrete götür
Özün gibi bir er getir
Hiç cihana gelmez ola

- 53 -

WHAT'S NEEDED

To submit to a King's needed,
Never unreachable must be.
To brace to a threshold's needed,
No one can take away must be.

To be a bird and fly's needed.
To pass to a side is needed.
To drink from a sherbet's needed.
Drinker never sobers must be.

A quick sailor to be is needed.
To dive into a sea's needed.
To dig out a jewel's needed,
Unknown by the merchants must be.

To enter a garden's needed.
Pleasant recreation's needed.
To smell of a rose is needed,
That rose never can fade must be.

One to be a lover's needed.
To find the Beloved's needed.
To burn in fire of love's needed.
To burn in fire no more must be.

Yunus, now go and do sit down,
And your face to holiness turn.
A saint like your own essence bring,
Never has come to world must be.

- 54 -

BU YOLDA ACAİB ÇOK

Süretden gel sıfata yolda safa bulasın
Hayallerde kalmagıl yoldan mahrum kalasın

Bu yolda 'acaib çok sen 'acaib anlama
'Acaib anda ola dost yüzünü göresin

Aşk kuşağın kuşangıl dostun yolunu vargıl
Mücahede çekersen müşahede idesin

Bundan aşkın şehrine üç yüz deniz geçerler
Üç yüz deniz geçüben yedi Tamu bulasın

Yedi Tamu'da yangıl her birinde kül olgıl
Vücudun anda kogıl ayruk vücûd bulasın

Hakikatdir Hak şarı yedidir kapıları
Dergahında yüz türlü gerek kudret göresin

Evvelki kapısında bir kişi durur anda
Sana eydür teslim ol gel miskinlik bulasın

İkinci kapısında iki arslan vardır anda
Niçeleri korkutmuş olmasın kim korkasın

Üçüncü kapısında üç evren vardır anda
Sana hamle ederler olmasın kim dönesin

- 54 -

SEVEN DOORS *

From surface come to the core, thereof the meaning to find.
Remain not in illusion, lest from attained be deprived.

On this road strange is many, by strangeness do not be fooled.
May the only strangeness be, when the face of Friend you see.

Put on belt of love and come, reach the way of Friend and come.
If you do endure struggle, revelation may you see.

From here to city of love, they cross three hundred oceans.
Crossing three hundred oceans, the seven hells may you find.

In the seven hells do burn, in each one ashes become.
Your body there do give up, other body may you find.

City of God is for real, of its doors there are seven.
On the great door is written, "do enter, might to attain."

At its very first door, one person is on guard there.
He will say to you "come forth", may it not be that you go.

Standing at its second door, two lions are present there.
So many they have scared off, may it not be that you scare.

You will find at its third door, there will be three great snakes there.
They will attempt to attack, may it not cause your return.

Dördüncü kapısında dört pirler vardır anda
Bu söz rumuzdur gör kim delil bulasın

Beşinci kapısında beş ruhban vardır anda
Türlü meta'lar satar olmasın kim alasın

Altıncı kapısında bir Hur oturur anda
Sana eydür gel beri olmasın kim varasın

Çün kim anda varasın ol Huriyi alasın
Bir vayeden ötürü yoldan mahrum kalasın

Yedinci kapısında yediler oturur anda
Sana kurtuldun derler gir dost yüzün göresin

Çün içeri giresin dost yüzünü göresin
Ene'l-Hak şerbetini dost elinden içesin

Şu dediğim keleci vücuddan taşra değil
Tefekkür kılurısan cümle sende bulasın

Yunus işbu sözleri Hak varlığından eydür
İsteriysen kanını miskinlerde bulasın

You will find at its fourth door, there will be four elders there.
This word has hidden meaning, see that you find evidence.

You will find at its fifth door, five spirits will be present.
They will offer countless goods, may it not be you receive.

You will find at its sixth door, heavenly huri sitting there.
She will say to you "come forth" may it not be that you go.

For if you reach out to her, you take that heavenly huri.
Away from a benefit, left on the way you will be.

You will find at seventh door, seven will be sitting there.
They will tell you, you've been saved, enter for Friend's face to see.

For therein you will enter, countenance of Friend to see,
The sherbet of "Enel Hak",** from the hand of Friend to sip.

These things I am telling you are not outside the body.
If you do contemplation, you will find all within thee.

Yunus all these words herein, from the presence of Lord tells,
If you desire the well spring, you will find in selflessness.

* The Seven Chakras or Makams as they are called in Sufism
**Enel Hak: I am God

EY PADIŞAH

Ey Padişah-ı Lem Yezel
Y Kadir-ü Hayy-ü Ezel
Ey lutfu Çok Kahrı Güzel
Kahrın Da Hoş Lutfun Da Hoş

Aglatirsin zar zari
Eyer gostermezsen yari
Layik gorur isen nari
Narin da Hos nurun da Hos

Hoşdur Bana Senden Gelen
Ya Gonca Gül Yahut Diken
Ya Hil-a'tü Yahut Kefen
Askin da Hos Hukmun de Hos

Gerek Ağlat Gerek Güldür
Gerek Yasat Gerek Öldür
Aşık Yunus Sana Kuldur
Hayyin da Hos Mutun da Hos.

- 55 -

OH SULTAN

Oh Sultan who has no end.
Oh omnipotent giver of eternal life.
Oh full grace, lovely grief,
Pleasant your grace, so is your grief.

You make cry, and cry with hardship
If you don't reveal the beloved.
If you deem we deserve the fire
Pleasant your light, so is your fire.

Pleasant to me what comes from you,
Whether be rose bloom or a thorn,
A tailor made coat or a shroud,
Pleasant your love, so is your rule.

Whether make laugh or you make cry,
Whether make live or you make die.
Ashik Yunus is your subject.
 Pleasant your life, so is your death.

-56-

DERDIM BANA DERMAN

Ben dert ile ah ederdim,
Derdim bana derman imiş.
İster idim hasret ile,
Dost yanımda pinhan imiş.

Nerde diye fikrederdim,
Göğe bakıp şükrederdim
Dost benim gönlüm evinde,
Tenim içinde can imiş.

Sanırdım kendim ayrıyım,
Dost ayrıdır, ben gayrıyım.
Beni bu hayale salan,
Bu sıfatı hayvan imiş.

İnsan sıfatı kendi Hak,
İnsadadır Hak, doğru bak.
Bu insanın sıfatına,
Cümle âlem hayran imiş.

Her kim o insanı bile,
Hayvan ise insan ola.
Cümle yaradılmış kula,
İnsan dolu sultan imiş.

Tehvid imiş cümle âlem,
Tehvidi bilendir Adem.
Bu tevhidi inkar eden,
Öz canına düşman imiş.

-56-

MY TROUBLE WAS CURE TO ME

I used to whine with my troubles,
Turns out, my troubles were cure to me.
I used to desire him with a longing,
Turns out, secretly Friend was with me.

I used to wonder, asking where?
I used to look at the sky and pray.
Friend, in the house of my heart,
Turns out, was the life under my skin.

I used to think I was separate.
Friend is apart, I am different.
What put me in this illusion,
Turns out, was the animal in me.

The essence of human is God.
Image of God is human, look clearly.
To the countenance of this human,
Turns out, creation is in adoration.

Whoever gets to know this human,
If animal, will become human.
To all the created beings,
Turns out, man is filled with Sultan.

Turns out, all the realm is oneness.
The one who knows oneness is man.
Whoever denies this oneness,
Turns out, is a foe to himself.

İnsan olan buldu Hakk'ı,
Meclis onun, odur saki.
Hemen bu biçare Yunus,
Aşk ile aşina imiş.

The one who is human, found God.
He serves the drink at gathering.
Suddenly this wretched Yunus,
Turns out, is one and the same with Ashk.

EPILOGUE

Zât-ı Hakk'da mahrem-i irfân olan anlar bizi,

İlm-i sırda bahr-ı bî-pâyân olan anlar bizi.

Bu fenâ gülzârına bülbül olanlar anlamaz,

Vech-i bâkî hüsnüne hayrân olan anlar bizi.

Dünyâ vü ukbâyı ta'mir eylemekten geçmişiz,

Her taraftan yıkılıp vîrân olan anlar bizi.

Biz şol abdalız bıraktık eğnimizden şâlımız,

Varlığından soyunup üryân olan anlar bizi.

Kahr u lûtfü şey'i vâhid bilmeyen çeker azab,

Ol azabdan kurtulup sultân olan anlar bizi.

Zâhidâ ayık dururken anlamazsın sen bizi,

Cür'ayı sâfî içüp mestân olan anlar bizi.

Ârifin her bir sözünü duymaya insân gerek,

Bu cihânda sanmanız hayvân olan anlar bizi.

EPILOGUE

Those who are secretly enlightened in the Being of Truth understand us.
Those who are endless ocean in secret of knowledge understand us.

Those who are nightingales to this finite rose garden understand us not.
Those who are in adoration of the beauty of eternal face of God understand us.

We have given up on repairing the earth and the sky.
Those who are demolished at every side and devastated understand us.

We are such subjects of the Lord, we have shed our cloak from our back.
Those who have stripped themselves down and have become bare understand us.

Those who did not know grace and grief as one and the same, suffered.
Those who are freed from that suffering and have become Sultan understand us.

O pious, while sober you will understand us not!
Those who have drunk mouthful of purity and have become ecstatic understand us.

To hear every word of the attained takes a human.
In this world do not think those who are animal understand us.

Halkı koyup lâ mekân ilinde menzil tutalı,

Mısrıyâ şol canlara canân olan anlar bizi.

Ey Niyâzî katremiz deryâya saldık biz bugün,

Katre nice anlasın ummân olan anlar bizi.

Since we have placed ourselves in the direction of non existence,
Those who are beloveds to these souls understand us.

O Niyazi, we have released our drop into the ocean this day.
How could the drop understand, those who are ocean understand us.

MISRI Niyazi
Translated from Trkish by Öz Yağan

Book Bound by Megan Lambert, 2020

www.ingramcontent.com/pod-product-compliance
Lightning Source LLC
Chambersburg PA
CBHW032046090426
42744CB00004B/107